How to make management style more effective

W. J. Reddin

McGRAW-HILL Book Company (UK) Limited

London · New York · St Louis · San Francisco · Auckland
Bogotá · Guatemala · Hamburg · Johannesburg · Lisbon
Madrid · Mexico · Montreal · New Delhi · Panama
Paris · San Juan · São Paulo · Singapore · Sydney
Tokyo · Toronto

Other books by the same author

The Best of Bill Reddin
Management Effectiveness and Style—Individual or Situation
Effective Situational Diagnosis
Effectiveness Areas
The Money Book
Effective MbO
Managerial Effectiveness

Published by
McGRAW-HILL Book Company (UK) Limited
MAIDENHEAD · BERKSHIRE · ENGLAND

British Library Cataloguing in Publication Data
Reddin, Bill
  How to make your managerial style more
  effective.
  1. Management   2. Business
  I. Title
  658   HD31

  ISBN 0-07-084928-5

Library of Congress Cataloging-in-Publication Data
Reddin, W. J. (William J.)
  How to make your management style more effective.
  Includes index.
  1. Executive ability.   I. Title.
HD38.2.R43   1987   658.4′09   86-20074

ISBN 0-07-084928-5

12345 WL8987

Typeset by Eta Services (Typesetters) Limited, Beccles, Suffolk
and printed and bound in Great Britain by Whitstable Litho Limited,
Whitstable, Kent

Contents

Preface

The aim of this book is to help individual managers become more effective. While this will lead naturally to the organization becoming more effective, the main focus is on the individual manager. This planned increase in effectiveness will arise naturally from better understanding of the real nature of managerial effectiveness. The increase in effectiveness will also give greater insight into one's own strengths or weaknesses and the proven guidelines concerning improving managerial style through either changing situations or using the right style in them.

This book will be useful to the individual manager who uses it alone. It is also designed to be used on a team basis or in the context of some kind of developmental or training exercise.

It is fair to say that all of the ideas in this book have been well tested. I have been working for over 25 years in the area of managerial styles and mangerial effectiveness and have had these ideas tested on hundreds of thousands of managers in many countries.

The book stresses application. It gives direct guidelines on how to change one's own style, to understand better what gives rise to it, to analyse situations in more detail and to be far more precise about how to measure one's own effectiveness. There is little point in changing one's style if one is not clear what one's true effectiveness outputs should be.

Effectiveness is the central issue in management. It is the manager's job to be effective. It is the only job. The manager may be a supervisor of a production line or of an office pool, a newly appointed manager, a middle manager or the managing director. For that matter, these ideas apply as well to government officers, military generals and bishops.

There is an enormous confusion about effectiveness. Some writers go so far as to claim that it cannot be measured. Some managers measure themselves on what they do rather than what they achieve. Some people think that effectiveness has something to do with 'trying hard'. Effectiveness is not efficiency. Effectiveness is doing the right things, not doing things right.

I am totally committed to the idea of common sense in management. The only problem with common sense in management is that it is not common. Sometimes, I must admit, I introduce a bit of jargon here and there but the jargon is intended to clarify rather than confuse. As an example, there is a dimension in much psychological management literature which is silly. It proposes that there are two types of people, the rigid and the flexible. The argument runs that the rigid are the bad ones and the flexible are the good ones. That has not been my observation. I know many 'flexible' managers who change their minds to keep the peace and therefore are less effective. I call this style drift. I also know many 'rigid' managers who maintain a single style appropriately and are highly effective. I call this style resilience. So the addition of the jargon terms, style drift and style resilience, enables me to make it clear that style flexibility and style drift are not the same thing and that style rigidity and style resilience are not the same thing either.

In the very early 1960s I cut my teeth on managerial styles in North America. Styles were all the rage then, with an emphasis on relationships orientation. We all believed that democracy was inevitable in organizations. A few theories, all from the United States, proposed a single ideal style as the best style. When I first heard this proposed about 25 years ago I did not accept it. It did not fit things I knew to be true. I base my understanding on my experience and not on a trumped-up set of footnotes which can usually prove anything. I have had no reason to change my mind since. The ideal style myth simply has to go away, though apparently it will not in the United States at least. There will always be those around who prefer hope to reality. That is why *In Search of Excellence* was so well received.

While this book, like many books, may be dipped into at any point, I think there is some merit, with this book, in starting at the front and working one's way through. For instance, one must understand what effectiveness is before even thinking about changing one's style. If one does not know about effectiveness one has no idea what style one should use. In a similar way one needs to be able to make a better assessment of the situations before deciding how one should change one's style.

The whole thrust in this book is change in yourself, or you helping others to change, in order to improve effectiveness.

W. J. REDDIN

Acknowledgements

I would like to acknowledge the help of many people. Valerie Richardson and John Fry became 'book czars' to make sure we met the various production schedules. Joan Wilson provided great help with the earlier drafts and Angela Wood and Val Barratt the later ones. As usual, Claudia Maconick was hypersensitive to use of language. Keith Stewart and Charlie Chambre were helpful in sorting, storing, collating and retrieving various items. Too many organizations in too many countries have used the ideas in this book for one even to be able to begin to mention them. One company recently arranged a series of one-week seminars for their top 1750 managers, starting with the CEO, based on the ideas in this book. Many individual managers have also benefited. If the book is practical it is because practical people have helped me make it that way.

All unattributed quotations at the beginning of chapters are taken from my own writings.

Dedication

This book is dedicated to Colin Ward, CEO of Atlas Air Australia Pty Ltd, who fully understands the use of effective managerial styles to improve organization effectiveness and personal satisfaction in managerial work.

PART 1

Introduction

The objectives of this part are to introduce you to how the book can make you more effective, to give you an overview of the model on which the book is based and to give you an opportunity to complete a test which will measure your managerial style.

1. How this book will make you more effective

> One of the great differences between the amateur and the professional is that the latter has the capacity to progress.
>
> *W. Somerset Maugham*

> Life is not long, and too much of it must not pass in idle deliberation how it shall be spent.
>
> *Samuel Johnson*

This book will provide many opportunities for you to learn to improve your effectiveness. As we are all different, and all learn differently, you will obviously get more value from some parts of the book than from others. The essential point is, though, that the book is so written that it covers a fairly wide range of things to do. It may be that you will improve your effectiveness by an improved understanding of what managerial effectiveness really is; that you will understand better how to analyse situations to adapt to them and to change them; or that you will become more effective by increasing the use of your more effective styles and decreasing your use of less effective styles. Here is an outline of ways in which the book may help you. Again, some of these ways you will find more helpful than others.

An understanding of managerial effectiveness

Reading this book will provide you with a greatly increased understanding of managerial effectiveness. It can be clearly defined in any job that is needed and it is always measurable. This point is not understood by many. Too many managers think that their jobs consist of activities such as planning, scheduling and staffing. No managerial job is created to achieve these things. These are simply inputs to the job, not the outputs. Chapter 4, 'You and Your Managerial Effectiveness', makes it possible for you to see your job in output terms. There is little point in raising the issue of how you might change your style unless you understand clearly how you should measure your effectiveness; it would be like trying to create change in a vacuum. All of the examples in Chapter 4 are taken from real life. Little attention is given to easily clarified jobs such as those in production, marketing and sales. The more difficult examples chosen indicate that the idea of managerial effectiveness is applicable to all managerial jobs.

Self-awareness

Self-change, and change in others, must start with self-awareness. If you do not know where you stand, how can you truly evaluate where others are? If you think you are a heavily relationships manager when in fact you are a heavily task manager this will cause you many confusions and lead you to do the wrong things and to interpret things incorrectly. We do not have to go back to Socrates, who wrote 'Know thyself', but it is not a bad place to start. In this book your self-awareness will be increased fairly sharply through a variety of means. The first is by the test you are asked to complete in Chapter 3. This test measures the relative strength of your eight managerial styles. The later chapters go into the styles in some detail so that you will get a clear understanding of what the styles mean and your use of them. Effective managers need to be able to clearly recognize their own style and the style of others. Some managers are absolutely shocked when they suddenly realize that one of their subordinates moved to desertion some years ago and has stayed there. They had not thought about it that way. Some managers are astonished when they find that they are basically bureaucrats and this accounts for most of their problems.

Increasing your situational sensitivity

Once you have a better idea of where you are you can easily improve your ability to read situations for what they really contain. Some people distort. They bring a lot of ideas to every situation and recite these ideas rather than read the situation. People are different and situations are different. There are many popular forms of distortions and you may see yourself in one or more of them as they are described in this book. There are four quite different types of situations, each of which requires one of four quite different styles if the situation is to be managed effectively. You will obtain a clear understanding of these. In addition, situations contain up to 20 quite distinct elements. These elements are such things as superior,

subordinates, planning, need for creativity, need for change introduction and concern for errors. In some situations one element is by
far the most dominant and should be given the most attention. In
other situations there will be several elements which must be
balanced if the situation is to be understood and managed.

Increasing your style flexibility

In some situations style flexibility can be a key. You may have to
change your style to meet the many different elements in the
situation. But not always: in other situations style resilience is the
key, in others yet the trick in managing the situation effectively is to
choose a single style and stick to it. Obviously, style awareness and
situational sensitivity must precede the decision as to how flexible
you should be, and with respect to which situational elements. It
must be clear that an effective manager must adapt to the situation
which exists, or change it. Managerial style is an essential ingredient
in effective management. The style you use with your coworkers,
subordinates or superior, or the style by which your organization is
run, is very important indeed. We all know the popular style terms
such as autocrat and bureaucrat and many others; what is needed is
a clear definition of which styles are effective and which styles are
not. As always, it depends upon the situation.

Increasing your situational management skills

While managers must sometimes adapt to the situation, in other
cases the opposite is true. They must instead change the situation in
which they find themselves. This may be by changing subordinate
expectations about the way they should behave. It may be by a
change in work technology. It may be by changing the measurement
method. New brooms do not always sweep clean but sometimes they
do. This is situational management in action. Some managers use
too much of it unnecessarily and some use too little. Situational
management is often no more than overcoming resistance to change
to achieve a certain objective the manager has. Many hints in this
book will provide guidelines on identifying resistance and choosing
the best methods to overcome it: situational management in action.

2. Ideas on which this book is based

Make a model before building.

A. N. Whitehead

There is nothing so practical as a good theory.

K. Lewin

This book is based on some straightforward ideas. Some might call these a model, some might call them a theory, but let's just call them ideas. They are all outlined here so that you know where the book stands and where it goes. Clearly, managers must be concerned first with effectiveness, next with the situation in which this effectiveness must occur and then with the style they must use as an input to the situation to create the effectiveness. This idea is shown in Exhibit 2.1, which can be read either right to left or left to right. If it is read

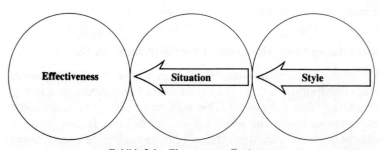

Exhibit 2.1   *The route to effectiveness*

from the right, managerial behaviour can be seen as an input to a situation that exists. Depending on whether the style is appropriate or not, effectiveness will or will not occur. It is equally well read in the other direction. Everything starts with effectiveness. When you settle that, you then analyse the situation and then you decide the most appropriate style of behaviour.

So, as an overview for this book, let us look at each of the three elements shown in Exhibit 2.1.

Effectiveness

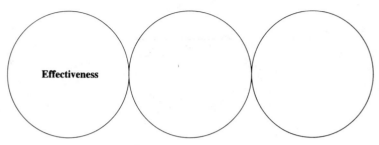

Exhibit 2.2   *Effectiveness*

This is covered in detail in Chapter 4 but here is an outline. There is only one definition of managerial effectiveness and that is 'the extent to which a manager achieves the output requirements of the position'. This definition hinges only on how well one can define outputs for all needed jobs. This can be completely defined but here is the general idea to start with:

INPUTS VS. OUTPUTS

- Maintain machines   *to*   • Machine availability
- Teach skills   *to*   • Skills usage
- Church attendance   *to*   • Values and behaviour change
- Customer satisfaction *to*   • Repeat sales

Maintaining machines is an input. But why do it? Obviously for machine availability. That is the output. Why teach any skill? Not for the fun of it: we do it only if the skill is used; in short, behaviour change. Why would you go to church? For the sake of it? Or for improved values and behaviour change? As an easy one, the output is not customer satisfaction but repeat sales. So, the definition of managerial effectiveness will be based upon outputs, not inputs. We need to learn just exactly how to specify an output; it is essential to improving effectiveness.

Situation

We are now moving to the second element, situation. How does one define a situation? Some of them demand a highly related type of behaviour. Some require a highly dedicated kind of behaviour which focuses on the job to be done in the short term. Some jobs, though managers find it hard to accept at times, require highly bureaucratic

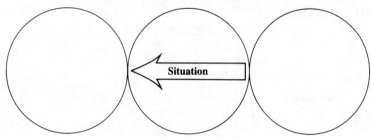

Exhibit 2.3 *Situation*

behaviour; that is, maintaining the system as it is. Some quite opposite situations require an integrated type of behaviour which involves a high level of interaction between managers, subordinates and work.

All managerial situations can be easily broken down into 20 elements. Some of these concern people, some the process to achieve productivity and some the interaction between people and productivity. Certainly, not all of them are important in all situations. Some are clearly more important in some situations than others. In some situations only one is important. Some managers could quite easily say that the central element in their situation is their superior. Others might say that it is controlling errors. Here are the 20 situational elements which will be discussed in more detail in Chapter 5.

Role set

1. Superior
2. Coworkers
3. Subordinates
4. Staff advisers
5. Unions
6. Customers
7. General public

Productivity set

8. Creativity
9. Objectives
10. Planning
11. Change introduction
12. Implementation
13. Controls
14. Evaluation
15. Productivity

Interaction set

16. Communication
17. Conflict
18. Errors
19. Meetings
20. Teamwork

Situations are analysed by deciding which elements are important so that you know with which elements it is important to be relatively effective. You cannot be absolutely effective with everything and sometimes one thing must be balanced against the other. You need to appraise the style demands being made in each of these elements. If your superior wants you to act in a bureaucratic fashion and has 100 per cent power over you then it seems fairly obvious what you must do to be effective in the superior's eyes, if not in your own. There is more on this in Chapter 5.

Style

The third major item to think about is behaviour, sometimes called management style. It is fairly well established in academic and

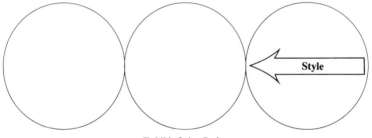

Exhibit 2.4 *Style*

management circles that there are two basic orientations towards the style a manager might use. One is either a high or a low task orientation and the other is a high or low relationships orientation. These are independent of each other so one can be high on both, low on both or high on one or the other. This leads to the notion of four basic styles as shown in Exhibit 2.5 based on task orientation (TO) as the horizontal dimension and relationships orientation (RO) as the vertical dimension.

Obviously these four basic styles match the four basic situations. The logic is that the style used must match the situation in order for effectiveness to be produced. If you are in a separated situation, one which demands a separated style, then use the separated style to be effective.

This leads to the notion of eight managerial styles, four less effective versions of the basic styles and four more effective versions

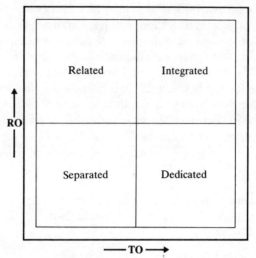

Exhibit 2.5   *Four basic styles of behaviour*

of the basic styles. This is introduced in Chapter 6 and each style is the subject of Chapters 7 to 14.

The logic of this basic argument leads to the knowledge that there are three basic managerial skills, as shown in Exhibit 2.6. The first skill, which must precede the other two, is the ability to read the situation for what it really contains, which is situational sensitivity. This leads to two choices. One is to change the situation, which is situational management. The other is to change yourself, which is style flexibility.

So that is the overview of the book. It is purely conceptual and does not give hints. The rest of the book will.

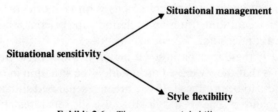

Exhibit 2.6   *Three managerial skills*

These three skills are the subject of Chapters 16 to 18.

3. Management style diagnosis test

Know thyself.
Socrates

The Management Style Diagnosis Test is designed solely for use by managers such as yourself. It enables you to look closely at your unique style of on-the-job behaviour and will provide you with valuable insights about it. The test is directly related to the eight styles of the 3-D theory of managerial effectiveness and has been widely tested in business, government and universities in many countries. Over 500 000 managers have taken it. The test will take you about thirty minutes or less to answer.

Instructions

1. The individual score sheet, Exhibit 3.1, has boxes numbered 1 to 56. These are used to record your choice from each pair of statements, also numbered 1 to 56, in the questionnaire.

   Look at the 56 pairs of statements in the questionnaire, Exhibit 3.2 on pages 14–17. If you think the first statement of a pair is the one that best applies to you, put an A in the appropriate box. If you think the second statement is the one that best applies to you, put a B. When you have finished, every box will contain either an A or a B.

   Notice that the boxes are numbered in sequence across the page; therefore, you should fill in the top line first, the second line next and so on.

   Example
   The first pair of statements is:

   A I do not show too much interest in maintaining good relationships with those above me.
   B I overlook violations of any kind if it helps to make things run more smoothly.

	1	2	3	4	5	6	7	
		1	2	3	4	5	6	7 —— A
8		9	10	11	12	13	14	—— B
15	16		17	18	19	20	21	—— C
22	23	24		25	26	27	28	—— D
29	30	31	32		33	34	35	—— E
36	37	38	39	40		41	42	—— F
43	44	45	46	47	48		49	—— G
50	51	52	53	54	55	56		—— H

Total Bs —— —— —— —— —— —— —— ——

Total As —— —— —— —— —— —— —— ——

A	B	C	D	E	F	G	H	
——	——	——	——	——	——	——	——	⎰ Total of this row should be 56

Adjustment factors   0   +2   0   0   0   −1   0   −1

Adjusted score —— —— —— —— —— —— —— —— ⎰ Total of this row should be 56

Exhibit 3.1   *Individual score sheet*

If you think that statement A is a better description of your behaviour than B, write A in the first box. If you think that statement B applies, put B in the first box. To decide which statement best applies, ask yourself: 'Of the two statements given, which best describes what I actually do on the job I now have?' It may be helpful, in difficult cases, to answer as someone would who really knew and understood your present approach to your job. Some statements you may find a little ambiguous, sometimes both will apply, often neither will seem to apply. However, in every case pick the one statement that would best describe you at present if you were faced with the circumstances described.

2. Total your As in each horizontal row and write the number alongside the row.
3. Total your Bs in each vertical column. Write the total below its column. Transfer the total of the As from step 2 just above the letters A–H.
4. Add each pair of numbers to give eight totals.
5. These eight numbers are your raw scores for the eight styles. (Together they should equal 56.)
6. Then add or subtract the adjustment factors indicated beneath to get eight new totals. These are your adjusted scores. Each will be interpreted when the eight styles are discussed.

(*See Exhibit 3.2 over*)

A	B
1 I do not show too much interest in maintaining good relationships with those above me.	I overlook violations of any kind if it helps to make things run more smoothly.
2 I do not always show a lot of interest in my subordinates.	I evaluate individuals personally. I frequently point out their good and bad points and criticise where necessary.
3 I believe the value of creativity, change, and innovation is often overemphasized.	I have some interest in high productivity but it is not always apparent and thus productivity sometimes suffers.
4 I think that the idea of setting overall objectives can be overdone.	I prefer to write out communications with others.
5 I think that planning can be overemphasized.	When conflict arises I always help those involved to find a basis for agreement.
6 I think that the actual introduction of a change imposed from outside should require only a moderate effort on my part.	I am certain that the best way to eliminate errors is for those making them to have their errors explained to them in detail.
7 I do not seem as interested as I might be in the actual implementation of decisions.	I actively support and promote the team approach to management.
8 I try to avoid disagreements with higher management even though this may lower my own or my subordinates' productivity.	I believe that evaluation and review are often overstressed.
9 I treat subordinates with great kindness and consideration.	I seem more interested in day to day productivity than in long run productivity.
10 I think that some new ideas lead to disagreement and friction.	While I do try to keep an open channel of communication with others, I am sometimes unsuccessful in doing so.
11 I allow subordinates to set their own objectives according to their needs and accept them even if somewhat unsatisfactory.	I respond to disagreement and conflict by referring to rules and procedures.
12 I prefer to let each individual make their own plans as long as they are clear.	I think that most errors arise for a good reason and it is always better to look for the reason than at the error itself.
13 I prefer to introduce change slowly rather than rapidly.	I believe a strong team needs a strong leader who knows what to do.
14 I tolerate deviations in implementing plans if this will avert unpleasantness.	If a procedure or control is violated I make sure I concentrate on finding out why.
15 I prefer to do my job with no interference from those above.	I am not too interested in improving productivity just for its own sake.

Exhibit 3.2 *Management style diagnosis test questionnaire. You should read across from column A to column B.*

	A	B
16	I direct the work of my subordinates and discourage deviations from my plans.	I communicate with others so as to maintain a good relationship above all else.
17	I think new ideas from below are sometimes less useful than those from above.	When conflict arises I am always fair and firm.
18	Deviations from the specific objectives I set for others are discouraged.	I believe that errors would be minimal if people simply followed established rules and procedures.
19	I see planning as a one-person job.	I believe in the team approach to the extent that I think all problems are best solved that way.
20	I think a good way to introduce change is to make an announcement and then let people get on with it.	I show that I think tough control techniques are among the most important aids to high productivity.
21	I watch implementation of plans closely, point out errors and criticise where necessary.	I have both methods and output under constant review and changes in them are regularly implemented as needed.
22	I want to improve my relationships with superiors but do not always take the action necessary.	I could supply more useful information to others than I do.
23	When dealing with subordinates I attempt to combine both task and relationships considerations but one or the other often suffers.	At the first sign of conflict I attempt to smooth things over.
24	I sometimes encourage new ideas but do not always follow up on too many of them.	I believe that when an error occurs the person responsible should be reprimanded.
25	While my objectives are usually fairly clear, I allow them to be quite loose so that they are not always a good guide.	I think that the team approach is of use at times but that formal meetings accomplish as much or even more.
26	I make an effort at planning but the plans do not always work out.	I believe that performance data is best fed back to the individual concerned rather than to a superior or a staff unit.
27	I sometimes talk about the problems of introducing change but do not always attempt to deal with these problems.	I keep methods and output under constant review and make changes to ensure high output.
28	I keep an eye on the implementation of plans but do not always take action when it is most needed.	I set high standards for myself and encourage others to set high output standards.
29	I believe that there will be few problems between myself and higher management if proper procedures and channels are followed.	I avoid conflict even when facing it could be useful.

A	**B**
30 I think that things go best when subordinates understand and follow the duties in their job descriptions.	I believe that if an error occurs it should be corrected in such a way that no one will be upset.
31 I believe that formal meetings are a perfectly sound way to produce new ideas.	I believe in 'One Person, One Job, Well Done.'
32 The objectives I set are usually fairly clear though somewhat inflexible.	I say that I believe control techniques are useful but I establish few and violate some.
33 I plan with a fine attention to detail.	I encourage others to evaluate their own and my own performance.
34 I introduce changes formally and follow closely any established procedures.	I personally set high output standards for myself and others and work hard to see that they are met.
35 Once plans are made I try to ensure their implementation follows the original plan.	I have an open communication channel with everyone on any matter and others have it with me.
36 I understand and co-operate well with higher level management.	I show little concern about errors and usually do little to correct or reduce them.
37 My relationship with subordinates is excellent and is characterized by mutual trust and respect.	I believe that team meetings are good primarily because they get people to talk together more.
38 I always seek out new and good ideas and motivate others to be as creative as possible.	I sometimes object to what I believe are unnecessary procedures.
39 I successfully motivate others to set their own clear objectives.	I talk about the importance of evaluation and review but do not always get involved with it myself as much as I might.
40 When I am responsible for planning I involve many others.	I believe that the best measure of output is a comparison based on norms previously established.
41 I prepare those affected by change by talking with them well in advance.	I keep everyone fully informed of what I think they need to know in order to do their job better.
42 I am responsive to sound proposals for modifying plans, am open to suggestions, and am always willing to help.	I try to resolve conflict as quickly as possible by uncovering its underlying causes.
43 I work well with higher level management and ensure that they know exactly how I see my job.	I think control procedures can be overdone.
44 I make it quite clear to subordinates what I expect of them. I show that I value efficiency and productivity.	I believe that the proper treatment of people is the best way to get productivity.

Exhibit 3.2 (*continued*)

	A	**B**
45	I both develop and propose many new ideas.	When disagreement arises I usually take a firm but understanding stand.
46	I personally set clear objectives that are understood by all those involved.	I like the idea of team work but often am not able to find ways to apply it.
47	I plan well and concentrate primarily on my own good ideas and assign individual responsibilties.	I emphasize regular evaluation, measurement and review of performance.
48	I inform all concerned of the reason for a change.	I maintain open trusting communication channels with everyone.
49	I watch the implementation of plans by individuals and give direct assistance and guidance where needed.	I treat errors primarily as opportunities for everyone to learn and am prepared to look openly at my own errors.
50	I believe higher management is simply another team that should co-operate effectively with teams lower down.	I have a few doubts about the team approach to management but would give it a trial if the situation was appropriate.
51	I consistently obtain high output from my subordinates.	I believe it is sometimes necessary to say that a satisfactory job has been done when it was not really all that was expected.
52	I am constantly on the watch for new, useful and productive ideas from any source and develop many new ideas myself.	I sometimes 'shoot down' the ideas of others.
53	I set objectives with others which are clear and fully agreed to by all those directly involved.	I believe that one can learn from errors and that I should show it more in my behaviour.
54	When I am involved the plans made represent the best thinking of all concerned.	I believe that controls are an important element in obtaining productivity.
55	I inform all concerned well in advance of any possibe changes and give them an opportunity to influence the proposed change.	I motivate others to set high output standards and encourage and support them so that these high standards are met.
56	I keep an eye on the implementation of plans and respond quickly to, and solve, any blockages.	When facing disagreement I try to be as persuasive as possible.

PART 2

Effectiveness, situation and style

This part consists of three chapters which go into detail on the basic elements underlying this book. We start where we must start. Obviously, effectiveness must come first. Knowing that, we can then think about other things. Effectiveness occurs in a situation. We need to be able to make a better analysis of situations. Managers behave in situations in order to improve effectiveness. So then we look at style.

4. You and your managerial effectiveness

CEOs should be paid according to the amount of time they could remain dead in their office with no one noticing. If a long time, it means they are concentrating on low frequency, long range decisions, which is what they are being paid for.

Effectiveness is the central issue in management. It is the manager's job to be effective. It is the only job.

The objective of this chapter is to help you to think about how you should measure your effectiveness. You may already have a very clear idea and again you may not. Obviously we start with effectiveness because if you are confused about how to measure your effectiveness and outputs generally, then, by definition, you have to be confused about everything else. If you do not know what your outputs are, how ever can you decide how to improve your managerial style?

There really is only one realistic and unambiguous definition of managerial effectiveness: it is 'the extent to which a manager achieves the output requirements of the position'. This definition hinges on a clear understanding of what output means; once it is understood and accepted it can easily lead directly to you deciding to change your behaviour. It is quite possible that you are focusing on inputs and activities, thus driving yourself to acting more like a bureaucrat, when in fact you should act more like a benevolent autocrat or some other more effective style.

Three types of effectiveness

There are three types of effectiveness. To understand what managerial effectiveness really is it is necessary to differentiate it clearly from the other two kinds, apparent effectiveness and personal effectiveness.

Managerial effectiveness

Managerial effectiveness is not an aspect of personality. It is not something a manager has. To see it as something a manager has is nothing more or less than a return to the now discarded trait theory of leadership. This theory suggested that more effective leaders had special qualities not possessed by less effective leaders. Effectiveness is best seen as something a manager produces in a situation by behaving in it appropriately. In current terminology it represents output, not input. The manager must think in terms of performance, not personality. It is not so much what managers do, but what they achieve.

Apparent effectiveness

It is quite important for you to be able to distinguish managerial effectiveness from apparent effectiveness. Apparent effectiveness is the extent to which a manager looks effective. Some descriptions that make people simply look effective include:

- Usually on time
- Answers promptly
- Makes quick decisions
- Liked by subordinates
- Good communicator
- Good at public relations
- Writes clearly

While these qualities may be useful in some jobs at some times they give absolutely no indication of level of managerial effectiveness. They only point to a level of what seems to be effectiveness to the naive observer. Behaviour must be evaluated in terms of whether or not it is appropriate to the output requirements of the job. In short, apparent effectiveness may or may not lead to managerial effectiveness. There may be little wrong with the items listed above but they do not necessarily point to managerial effectiveness.

Conventional job descriptions often lead to an emphasis on what could be called managerial efficiency, the ratio of output to input. The problem is that if both input and output are low, efficiency can still be 100 per cent. In fact, a manager or department can easily be 100 per cent efficient and 0 per cent effective.

Efficient managers are easily identified. They prefer to:

- Do things right   *rather than* ● Do right things

- Solve problems   *rather than*   • Produce creative
                                           alternatives
- Safeguard resources *rather than*   • Optimize resource
                                           utilization
- Discharge duties   *rather than*   • Obtain results

Conventional job descriptions lead to the apparent effectiveness of the behaviour as listed in the left column; a job effectiveness description which emphasized managerial effectiveness would lead to performance as listed in the column on the right.

The distinction between managerial effectiveness and apparent effectiveness can be further illustrated by what really happens when a 'steamroller' manager brings what appears to be chaos to an organization but the situation clearly begins to improve. Unless outputs are the focus of attention, the result can be a serious distortion of what is really going on.

Personal effectiveness
Personal effectiveness is related to achieving your own personal objectives. These may include keeping your job, a preferred career route, larger office, larger desk, bigger budget, feeling good and winning arguments. All these are in the service of personal needs. Like the indicators of apparent effectiveness, they may or may not contribute to managerial effectiveness. Some organizations promote on the basis of apparent effectiveness. Some promote on the basis of personal effectiveness. This is particularly likely to occur with ambitious people in an organization having only a few closely defined management output measures. Meetings with these people are riddled with hidden agendas which operate below the surface and lead to poor decision making.

There is nothing necessarily wrong with either personal effectiveness or apparent effectiveness. We all like to make it in our own terms and we all like to appear effective. The problem arises only when either condition is confused with managerial effectiveness and substituted for it. It is important to note that in a well-designed firm all three kinds of effectiveness can occur simultaneously for any particular manager. This would mean that managers who are in fact effective (managerial effectiveness) look as if they are effective (apparent effectiveness) and are rewarded for it in their own terms (personal effectiveness). We should try to design more organizations that way but first always must come managerial effectiveness.

The deadly sin of inputs

The first step in your becoming more effective is to think even more about your job in output terms. These outputs of jobs are generally referred to as effectiveness areas. Jobs tend to have five or ten of them. They must all be outputs. The problem is however that too many jobs are described in terms of inputs, not outputs: in terms of input areas and not in terms of effectiveness areas.

The source of some of the problems which surround effectiveness is found in the way job descriptions are written. Lengthy job descriptions, or even crash programmes to write or update them, usually have little actual usefulness. As C. Northcote Parkinson has pointed out, the last act of a dying organization is to issue a revised and greatly enlarged rule book. This observation may hold just as well for crash programmes to write job descriptions.

Many, if not most, managerial jobs are defined in terms of their input and behaviour requirements by such phrases as: 'administers'... 'maintains'... 'organizes'... 'plans'... 'schedules'. Naturally enough, managers never refer to job descriptions like these; once made, they are not very useful as an operating guide. They are often proposed initially by those who want to use a seemingly scientific technique to justify a widespread change in salary differentials or a change in the organization structure. They are often a negative influence, as they focus on input and behaviour, the less important aspects of the manager's job.

The most common error in setting effectiveness areas is in producing input areas instead. An input area is an incorrect statement of an effectiveness area which is based on activities or inputs rather than results or outputs.

Most inputs can be converted to outputs if the position is needed at all. Some examples were given on page 7 and here are a few .more:

- Insurance   *to* • Asset projection
- Coach subordinates   *to* • Subordinate effectiveness
- Train   *to* • Change behaviour
- Farmer education   *to* • High value crop acreage
- Speed reading   *to* • Speed learning

One should beware of such areas as communication, relationships, liaison, coordination and staffing: these areas usually suggest inputs.

Authority

Your outputs must be based on the authority you have. If you do not have the authority to achieve an output then you cannot take responsibility for it. Virtually no one in any situation has control of all the variance in an output. The key question to ask is, 'Do you have control of most of the variance in your organization?' Sometimes when brand managers get promoted to marketing managers the person that replaces them finds the recently promoted manager has taken some authority upwards. So the new brand manager, so called, really becomes a brand planner because the position does not give the opportunity to make changes in the product or to change prices. The main output could be simply producing plans, while the title suggests that it is producing profits. Producing plans, in this case, may be the output because the manager does not have the authority to go further.

The training officer

While many initial attempts to set effectiveness areas turn out instead to be a list of activities, many attempts can go in the other direction. Sometimes everyone appears to think they are heading a profit centre. Of any proposed effectiveness area the question should be asked, 'Why is this being done?' or 'Why is this important?' For example, training managers might go through the following kind of process. They are first asked what their most important area is, to which they might reply, 'To design a management development programme.' When asked, 'Why?' they reply, 'To put on courses for managers.' When again asked, 'Why?' they reply, 'To improve the quality of managerial decisions.' To yet another 'Why?' the reply is, 'To improve profit performance.' The correct area for these training managers would probably be 'To increase managerial skill in problem solving'. It cannot be 'To improve the quality of managerial decisions' or 'To improve profit performance' as these are both influenced by many factors over which the training managers have no control. They have no authority. On the other hand, the areas cannot be simply 'programme design' or 'putting on courses', which are clearly inputs.

So, in short, the way you find your outputs is to keep asking 'Why?' until you fall off the limit of your authority and cannot take responsibility for variance in the output that you have arrived at. If we all keep asking 'Why?' beyond this point we all end up with 'improving the gross national product'. Things have to stop somewhere. They stop at the limit of your authority.

In this chapter we have quite deliberately avoided easy examples such as in production and marketing and sales. Far more difficult ones are chosen. Surely, if the point can be made with the difficult ones then it should be reasonably straightforward to do it with the easy ones. Finding effectiveness areas is better done on a team basis: we all need a little help from our friends.

University director of physical education

A newly appointed university director of physical education with a staff of about ten produced the following as first and second attempts.

First attempt:

1. Character building
2. Health
3. Sports activity
4. Maintenance
5. Staffing
6. Future programmes

Second attempt:

7. Utilization of facilities
8. Readiness of facilities
9. Quality of facilities
10. Programme innovation rate
11. Growth of facilities

This director came to see that there could be only partial influence on areas 1 (character building) and 2 (health) and that there was no practical measuring device for the former (character building), that 3 (sports activity) and 4 (maintenance) were best expressed as 7 (utilization of facilities) and 8 (readiness of facilities), and that 5 (staffing) was an input and that 6 (future programmes) could be more clearly worded as 10 (programme innovation rate). Unlike some such managers, there was some control over the growth of facilities and it was thought appropriate to include 11 (growth of facilities).

Tests for effectiveness areas

All effectiveness areas should meet four tests:

- Output
- Measurability
- Importance
- Authority

Obviously, effectiveness areas must represent output not input. No less important, they must lead to associated objectives which are measurable. If you think your job has some element of nonmeasurability then simply forget it because no one will know anyway. All outputs are measurable. You may decide not to measure them because of the cost of measurement. The time needed to measure them might be several years. Neither of these points violates a basic idea of science that if something exists then it is measurable. Another test is importance. The reason for this is to avoid creating very long lists of effectiveness areas. Five to ten is usually enough. Stick to the important things, otherwise the list becomes unmanageable for planning purposes. Obviously, the output must be within your authority.

So, will you give some thought to how you will measure your effectiveness in output terms? Are you now making some of the mistakes which have been indicated here? Why not try the exercise of listing what you think your outputs are—they may turn out to be activities in some part—and asking 'Why?' until you realize you cannot control the variance? This kind of activity is quite definitely done best on a team basis as other people can contribute ideas and tend to be somewhat more objective.

5. You and your managerial situation

Once your effectiveness areas are better understood it is necessary to look at the managerial situation in which these outputs are to be achieved. Only then can you decide what behaviour should be used. The purpose of this chapter is to give you a sound framework for looking at your managerial situation. It will help you think about what behaviour is appropriate for you to improve your effectiveness in your situation. So, we are focusing on the second element: situation.

This chapter tackles the analysis of situations in three different ways. You may well find one method more helpful than the others, and all you need. You may find that all three help you. No matter what method you use, the objective remains the same: for you to derive how you should behave in a situation so that your effectiveness will be increased. The three methods are:

- Basic situation demand indicators
- Technology demand indicators
- Twenty situational elements

Four types of basic situation demands

Broadly speaking, your situation is demanding from you one of four types of behaviour. These derive from two underlying demands which are independent of each other: the demand that you be more or less task oriented (TO) and the demand that you be more or less relationships oriented (RO). As these two demands are independent it is straightforward to derive four basic types of behaviour demanded:

- *Separated* Low on task and relationships
- *Related* High on relationships, low on task
- *Dedicated* High on task, low on relationships
- *Integrated* High on both task and relationships

It is simply true that situations vary in what they demand in order for effectiveness to result. Some situations, often in production settings, require dedicated behaviour in order for effectiveness to result. Certainly, managing independent professionals, such as research and development scientists not working as a team, demands related behaviour in order for effectiveness to result.

Basic situation demand indicators

What do you think are the demands your managerial situation is making on your behaviour? Exhibit 5.1 gives some indicators of the five general demands for each of the four basic types of situation. You might look these indicators over and after you read the definitions below check off which ones you think your situation

	Related	Integrated
	1 To trust	1 To participate
	2 To listen	2 To interact
	3 To accept	3 To motivate
	4 To advise	4 To integrate
	5 To encourage	5 To innovate
RO	1 To examine	1 To organize
	2 To measure	2 To initiate
	3 To administer	3 To direct
	4 To control	4 To complete
	5 To maintain	5 To evaluate
	Separated	Dedicated

⟶ TO ⟶

Exhibit 5.1 *Indicators of situation demands*

demands of you in order for effectiveness to result. Later, we raise the broader issue of changing situational demands when we discuss situational management, but you might make some check marks now on the assumption that you cannot change your situation very much.

Here are explanations of what each of the 20 items means. Check those that apply in your situation.

SEPARATED DEMAND INDICATORS

Examine   The degree to which continual, careful, systematic and deliberate examination of material or documents of any kind is expected.

Measure   The degree to which a considerable amount of objective measurement or evaluation of any kind is expected.

Administer   The degree to which conscious and deliberate administration in accordance with existing principles, rules and procedures is expected.

Control   The degree to which close control is expected to avoid variations in any kind of plan, schedule, budget or design.

Maintain   The degree to which the primary expectation is the maintenance of records.

Which of these apply in your situation?

RELATED DEMAND INDICATORS

Trust   The degree to which absolute trust and open candid communication across departmental or status and power levels are expected.

Listen   The degree to which attentive, sincerely interested listening, sometimes over long periods, is expected.

Accept   The degree to which complete, active, genuine acceptance of other's motives and actions is expected even when sharply different from one's own.

Advise   The degree to which a considerable amount of helpful friendly advice is expected.

Encourage   The degree to which extensive approving and sympathetic encouragement is expected.

Which of these apply in your situation?

DEDICATED DEMAND INDICATORS

Organize The degree to which extensive planning and regular reorganization of work are expected.

Initiate The degree to which many new tasks are expected to be initiated independently.

Direct The degree to which a considerable amount of active direction of the work of others is expected.

Complete The degree to which it is expected that the primary consideration is to complete the immediate task at hand.

Evaluate The degree to which rigorous evaluation of performance is expected and appropriate action taken.

Which of these apply to your situation?

INTEGRATED DEMAND INDICATORS

Participate The degree to which it is expected that most decision making will be by fully participative methods.

Interact The degree to which a considerable amount of task-oriented interpersonal interaction is expected.

Motivate The degree to which considerable and approximately equal amounts of both relationships orientation and task orientation are expected.

Integrate The degree to which individual needs and organization goals are expected to be suitably balanced and seen as one.

Innovate The degree to which a very high number of original ideas concerning methods of improving both relationships and production is expected.

Which of these apply in your situation?

Looking at your situation broadly you will find it helpful to think about each of these 20 items and really ask yourself what behaviour is being demanded. In this way you will get an initial idea of how you should behave for effectiveness. The key question is, 'What behaviour is currently demanded for your effectiveness to be increased?' It may well be that your perception of the behaviour 'demanded' by your superior leads to less effectiveness rather than more effectiveness. If you cannot exercise situational management and change your superior's demands it may well be true that your superior is in fact driving you to less effectiveness and there is nothing you can do about it. This is not the normal case, though it is often perceived to be and sometimes is.

Work technology also influences style demands

You may well find that the indicators provided so far have helped you to understand the demands being made on your behavioural style. However, the analysis can go further. It is possible to look at the work technology itself to get an indicator of demands. You may find that looking at technology indicators as shown in Exhibit 5.2 will deepen your understanding of why certain demands arise.

The kind of work being done obviously indicates the style of

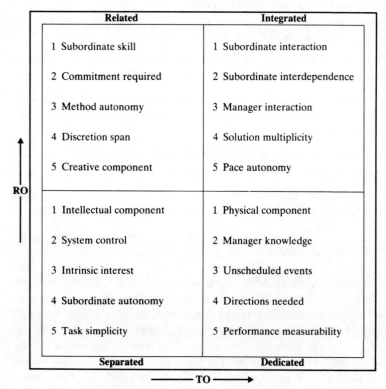

Exhibit 5.2 *Indicators of technology demands*

behaviour required. In batch production more of a dedicated style should be used. In continuous-flow production processes, with fixed stations, demands may be more separated or related. Managing an accounting department demands a different style from managing a group of office equipment sales staff. Work technology influences behaviour required to produce effectiveness. While work technology is only one element of many it is being presented here for special attention, because as a general case it has a major influence, though it may not in your situation.

You may find it useful to review each of these 20 indicators while thinking of the nature of the work in which you are involved. This is another way of looking at demands, focusing on the work alone rather than the elements in a situation such as superior, coworkers and subordinates.

There now follow explanations of what each of the 20 items mean. The precise question to ask yourself about these definitions is, 'Which of these 20 indicators best describes the actual current technology in my situation?' It is possible, but most unlikely, that you will find all five indicators apply in any one of the four basic demands and none in the others. It is more usual to find three in one, two in another and one in another. If, for instance, you have checked three in integrated and two in dedicated it indicates that your demands, on the basis of looking at the work technology only, are integrated and dedicated and it is around those two styles that you are likely to be more effective when thinking of work technology.

SEPARATED TECHNOLOGY INDICATORS

Intellectual component   Degree to which subordinates are required to think rather than to act.

System control   Degree to which subordinates' work and work method follow established procedures.

Intrinsic interest   Degree to which subordinates' work is in and of itself interesting, motivating or attractive.

Subordinate autonomy   Degree to which subordinates have discretion over their effectiveness standards.

Task simplicity   Degree to which subordinates' tasks are simple to perform.

Which of these apply in your situation?

RELATED TECHNOLOGY INDICATORS
Subordinate skill Degree to which position makes high skill or judgement demands on subordinates.

Commitment required Degree to which position requires the subordinates to be personally committed if all effectiveness standards are to be fully achieved.

Method autonomy Degree to which subordinates can select the method, tools or approach they wish to use.

Discretion span Degree to which time can elapse before substandard work of subordinates is detected.

Creative component Degree to which position requires subordinates to develop new methods and ideas.

Which of these apply in your situation?

DEDICATED TECHNOLOGY INDICATORS
Physical component Degree to which subordinates are required to use physical effort.

Manager knowledge Degree to which subordinates know less about the task than the manager.

Unscheduled events Degree to which unplanned and unanticipated events might occur which require corrective action by the manager.

Directions needed Degree to which subordinates need to be given directions frequently in order for them to complete their task.

Performance measurability Degree to which subordinates' performance is measurable, and the impact of remedial actions taken by the manager can be evaluated.

Which of these apply in your situation?

INTEGRATED TECHNOLOGY INDICATORS
Subordinate interaction Degree to which the subordinates must talk with each other to complete their task.

Subordinate interdependence Degree to which the subordinates must depend on each other in meeting their own effectiveness standards.

Manager interaction Degree to which the manager must talk with subordinates as a group for them to complete their tasks.

Solution multiplicity Degree to which more than one effective solution is possible, where relative effectiveness of these solutions is difficult to measure, and where the number and evaluation of solutions is improved by interaction.

Pace autonomy Degree to which subordinates may set their own pace, effort or involvement level.

Which of these apply in your situation?

Two exercises concerning technology demands
Here are two short exercises to get you to think more about technology demands. The two case studies are written up very briefly indeed. If they were each several pages long it is probable that most managers would agree fully on the technology demands. As there is a lot unsaid there is room for error. The rough answers are given at the end of the chapter. If you get about half right at this point you have a general understanding. If you get less than that then it might be worth while to study the definitions again. The 'answers' are on page 38.

Case study 1 This concerns a fixed station production system. The manager of the system is its supervisor. The work is the assembly of automobiles. There is a continuous moving belt which carries the automobiles to the supervisor's work area. The tasks in this area are highly specific. The tasks are repeated continuously. There are one supervisor and 300 employees in this work area. The question to be asked is, 'What demands is this work technology making on the supervisor in order for the supervisor to be more effective?' List the indicators given in Exhibit 5.2 which you think apply.

Case study 2 This concerns a specialist accounting service for doctors with private patients. Basically the responsibility is to collect bills that doctors have issued. The firm has 12 employees. The manager in this case is the CEO of the firm who actively supervises the work. They have 200 doctors as clients and give all of them daily reports generated on their own computer. Again, the question is, 'What demands is this work technology making on the supervisor in order for the supervisor to be more effective?' List the indicators given in Exhibit 5.2 which you think apply.

Twenty situational elements

This chapter provides you with three ways of looking at your situation. The first way proposed was to look at your situation globally and not at any particular element and consider what basic style is being demanded. The second method proposed was to look at the work technology alone and make the same kind of analysis. The third method is to look at the situation in a more particular way and select which of 20 elements are making the most demands on you and make the same kind of basic style demand analysis with those elements. As indicated in Chapter 2 and shown again in Exhibit 5.3, managerial situations can be seen to be composed of one

1 Superior	The person to whom you report
2 Coworkers	Managers of equivalent level or authority with whom you interact
3 Subordinates	Those who report directly to you
4 Staff advisers	Knowledge workers, usually with low authority and power, whose job it is to provide information and advice
5 Unions	Union representatives or members of unions
6 Customers	The purchasers of the company's products or services
7 General public	Anyone who is not an employee or customer of the company
8 Creativity	The production of ideas
9 Objectives	What you plan to achieve
10 Planning	The specific means whereby objectives are realized
11 Change introduction	The actual initiation of a new plan
12 Implementation	The actions taken to realize plans and decisions
13 Controls	Methods of monitoring actions so that adjustments can be made if necessary
14 Evaluation	Measurement of the effectiveness of action
15 Productivity	The level of the manager's output of those things required by the manager's superior
16 Communication	Receipt and transmission of information
17 Conflict	Disagreements
18 Errors	Things that go wrong
19 Meetings	Two or more people coming together to discuss something
20 Teamwork	Interaction between two or more people with high emphasis on both task and relationships orientations

Exhibit 5.3   *The twenty situational elements*

or more of 20 situational elements. In the average managerial situation one or two may be quite dominant and many will be absent.

The first seven of these elements are called role set elements as they refer generally to other people in their various roles. Elements 8 to 15 are meant to indicate the various steps from creativity, thinking about an idea, to eventually improving productivity. The steps are roughly sequential in that after one gets an idea (creativity), one sets objectives concerning it (objectives); one then makes plans to achieve the objectives (planning)—and so on. In some jobs some of these elements are more important than others. The last five elements, 16 to 20, all refer to some kind of interaction between people and work.

Element dominance

Some of these elements are dominant in your situation. By dominance is meant the degree to which they affect the style you should use to improve your effectiveness. You may find it useful to decide which of the 20 elements has most influence on you in determining the style you should use to improve your effectiveness, and to indicate the relative strength of these by assigning them ten points in all between them. In some cases you might put all the weight on one element but you would more likely spread the points over a few. This analysis can then help you focus on what demands each element in particular is making. For the more important elements you might want to return to either Exhibit 5.1 or Exhibit 5.2, or both, so that you can make a more particular analysis. This is not essential at this point.

Relative effectiveness

Looking at the elements to which you assigned some points, consider, right now, how effective you are with them. You might find it useful to have a scale from 0 to 4 to indicate this. Obviously, there will be a degree of subjectivity in your assessment but there is sufficient evidence to show that managers are quite capable of making a reasonable assessment themselves. It will make the analysis too detailed if you look at the relative effectiveness of all 20 elements: it is best to limit it to the ones to which you assigned some degree of dominance. However, the main thing is to think about your situation in a way that is helpful to you.

Summary

This chapter has given you three different ways to look at your situation. You may want to use one or more of them. They may produce fairly similar results or somewhat different ones. They will all, however, get you to think about your situation and the demands it is making on you in order for you to be effective. The assumption running through this chapter is that you must be flexible in responding to the demands you observe rather than changing them, but when we move on to situational management a quite different notion will be presented, namely that it might be best for you to change the demands rather than responding to them.

ANSWERS TO CASE STUDY ONE
The indicators that best seem to apply are:

Separated B and E.	*Related* —.
Dedicated A, C and E.	*Integrated* —.

ANSWERS TO CASE STUDY TWO
The indicators that best seem to apply are:

Separated B and E.	*Related* A.
Dedicated E.	*Integrated* B.

6. You and your managerial style

There is a definite style to the high quality of accomplishment that marks the exceptional manager.

Erwin Schell

The beginning of administrative wisdom is the awareness that there is no one optimum type of management system.

Tom Burns

The objective of this chapter is to get you to think about your current basic style of management and also the other basic styles available. You will then be able to think in detail about applying the correct basic style based on your analysis of your situation in order to increase effectiveness. So, we come to the last element: style.

Two orientations

As with the analysis of situations described on page 28, there has been a great deal of research, by many investigators, into managerial style. A point on which there is virtual agreement is that it is useful to think of managerial behaviour as having two orientations, task orientation and relationships orientation. The titles pretty well explain the terms themselves; however the definitions are as follows:

- *Task orientation (TO)* The extent to which managers direct their efforts; characterized by initiating, organizing and directing.

- *Relationships orientation (RO)* The extent to which a manager has personal job relationships; characterized by listening, trusting and encouraging.

As it happens, these two important dimensions of managerial behaviour are rather independent of each other. A manager can be high on one and low on the other, high on both or low on both. This leads to the kind of diagram shown in Exhibit 6.1.

As these two dimensions are independent one can derive four basic styles which mirror the four basic situational demands. These

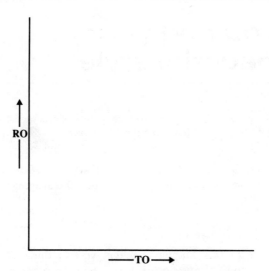

Exhibit 6.1   *Task and relationships orientation*

four basic styles represent managers who are separated from both task and relationships in their situations, others who are mainly related to others, others who are mainly dedicated to the job and finally others who have a major interest in integrating relationships and task.

Differences across the four basic styles

Obviously the four basic styles are very different. Exhibit 6.2 gives a clear indication of this. It is worth studying these differences in detail now and thinking about your own natural basic style.

Look at the first two lines. The interactional mode of the separated manager is correcting deviations. The related manager is accepting others. The dedicated manager tends to dominate and direct. The integrated manager wants to join with others in the service of work. The preferred mode of communication of the separated manager is written, as this involves less relationships orientation and can involve lower task orientation. The related manager obviously prefers to talk. The dedicated manager wants to give vocal directions as this helps domination. The integrated manager, rather obviously, prefers meetings.

You might now think about circling one item on each line. You may think about yourself two ways with this exhibit. One is how you prefer to behave because of your natural tendencies and the other how you should behave in your present situation to improve effectiveness. All managers bring to situations their natural propensities, however a professional manager is primarily concerned with serving what the situation demands, not serving self.

The separated style of manager

Separated managerial behaviour is characterized by both low task and low relationships orientation, i.e. behaviour literally separated from both people and task. The separated manager is really oriented to nothing changing, only to system maintenance (Exhibit 6.3).

SEPARATED MANAGER INDICATORS
- Cautious/careful/conservative
- Prefers paperwork
- Looks for established principles
- Accurate/precise/correct
- Steady/deliberate/patient
- Calm/modest/discreet

How separated managers differ

Separated managers have an orientation to procedures, methods and systems. Many highly intelligent and effective managers have a separated basic style.

Separated managers are ones who are very concerned about correcting deviations. They tend to write more than talk and partly because of this have relatively little personal communication in any direction. Their time perspective tends to be with the past and 'how we did it last time'. Thus they identify with the organization as a whole rather than with individual members of it. Because of their desire to keep things on an even keel they take great interest in the rules and procedures and naturally judge others on how well they adhere to them. They value intellect in their superiors but not necessarily in others. In committees they tend to use a subdued parliamentary style and attempt to clarify positions, guide others to work through the agenda, and channel all communications through the chair. They are obviously well suited to work in administration, accounting, statistics, engineering design, government and in the control departments of head offices.

	Separated	Related	Dedicated	Integrated
1 Interactional mode	Correcting	Accepting	Dominating	Joining
2 Mode of communication	Written	Conversations	Vocal directions	Meetings
3 Direction of communication	Little in any direction	Upwards from subordinates	Downward to subordinates	Two-way
4 Time perspective	Past	Unconcerned	Immediate	Future
5 Identifies with	Organization	Subordinates	Superior and technology	Coworkers
6 System emphasis	Maintains procedural system	Supports social system	Follows technological system	Integrates sociotechnical system
7 Judges subordinates on	Who follows the rules?	Who understands people?	Who produces?	Who wants to join the team?
8 Judges superior on	Brains	Warmth	Power	Teamwork
9 Committee activity	Clarifying, guiding and channeling	Supporting, harmonizing and coaching	Initiating, evaluating and directing	Setting standards, testing and motivating
10 Work suited for	Administration, accounting, statistics and design	Managing professionals, training and co-ordination	Production and sales management	Supervising interacting managers
11 Work not suited for	Nonroutine	Low personal contact	Low power	High routine
12 Employee orientation	Security	Co-operation	Performance	Commitment

	Separated	Related	Dedicated	Integrated
13 Reaction to error	More controls	Pass over	Punish	Learn from
14 Reaction to conflict	Avoids	Smothers	Suppresses	Utilizes
15 Reaction to stress	Withdraws and quotes rules	Becomes dependent and depressed	Dominates and exploits	Avoids making decisions
16 Positive source of control	Logic	Praise	Rewards	Ideals
17 Negative source of control	Argument	Rejection	Punishments	Compromise
18 Characteristic problem of subordinates	Lack of recognition	Lack of direction	Lack of information	Lack of independence
19 Punishments used	Loss of authority	Loss of interest by manager	Loss of position	Loss of self-respect by subordinates
20 Undervalues	Need for innovation	Needs of organization and of technology	Subordinates expectations	Need for independent action
21 Main weakness	Slave to the rules	Sentimentality	Fights unnecessarily	Uses participation inappropriately
22 Fears about self	Emotionality, softness and dependence	Rejection by others	Loss of power	Uninvolvement
23 Fear about others	System deviation irrationality	Conflict	Low production	Dissatisfaction

Exhibit 6.2 *Basic style differences*

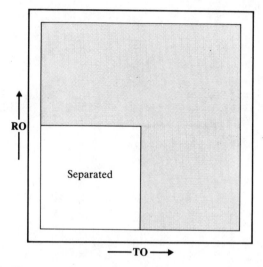

Exhibit 6.3   *The separated style. It has a low task orientation and a low relationships orientation*

The separated style may be induced by the relatively lengthy training programmes people in these positions often undergo, of which accountancy is the best example. The values induced in such training parallel the qualities of the separated style. There is the emphasis on accuracy, conservatism, prudence and noninvolvement.

Separated managers avoid nonroutine work because they do not enjoy it. When things go wrong their usual reaction is to propose more controls. This also helps to depersonalize future conflict, which they avoid if they can. When faced with conflict or other kinds of stress situations they tend to withdraw and quote rules and procedures. They value logic and rationality and are amenable to being influenced by it. The emphasis on logic can sometimes give way to argument, particularly if the problem could have been solved by relationships skills which they do not see as relevant. Their subordinates often believe that they do not recognize them or their accomplishments enough. They see their subordinates less as people and more as parts of their work system. Because of this they tend to punish by removing some of the authority previously given. They undervalue the need for innovation and are generally seen as slaves to the rules. The greatest fear they have about themselves is that they might let emotion, softness or dependence on others influence their judgement. Their greatest fear of others is that they might act irrationally and in some way violate the established system.

Separated managers often appear not too secure as people. Instead of interacting with their environment, they take refuge in the rules. They believe that if they follow the rules really well, they will not encounter too many difficulties. When confronted with decision making, separated managers want a clearly defined principle to follow. First they look at the written rules, for they go by the book. Then they will look at the customary ways of solving things in the past. Clearly this approach is useful, or even essential, for some positions in companies at some times. On the other hand, it may at times be quite inappropriate.

Impersonality

Separated managers are impersonal. This may at times be seen as arrogance and negativism, but it may also be seen as complete fairness and objectivity about people. Not only do they want to be seen as impersonal but they would also be very quick to complain about the slightest show of personal interest between their subordinates and those reporting to them. They suspect much helpfulness as favouritism. Separated managers will seldom be guilty of a tyranny of personal whims, though the tyranny of rigid rule application can be one of their major faults.

Separated managers are usually fair, not because of their relationships orientation but because of their lack of it. One way not to get involved is to treat everyone equally. This equality of treatment usually leads to emphasis on seniority rather than on ability.

Managing within change

Separated managers tend to drop in effectiveness as the amount of change required increases. They prefer specific instructions for each new situation, and until they get them they are against stretching rules just enough to keep all of them applicable. Clearly the separated style of management is highly inappropriate among key managers in a rapidly changing situation. A few separated managers such as accountants or lawyers, perhaps, may be of help in that situation, but most of the key figures cannot be separated because change will then not take place. Separated managers have an overwhelming need for symmetry and order. They want all the pieces to come together, all the numbers to be in place, and all the evaluations to be neatly tabulated. This is their bastion against change.

Increasing output, as such, does not really interest separated managers. They prefer to decrease costs rather than increase profit. This is one of many reasons why they are attracted to lower levels of the government service.

More so than with other basic styles, separated managers want others who are separated as subordinates. These managers will be tuned in to the same things as themselves, will add stability to their department, and influence and control in the name of procedures and existing system demands. They want subordinates to follow duties, not to follow the situation or them. They abhor strong personal leadership or example. The active, innovative subordinate will not work well with a separated superior. Their superior rewards them only for staying in line, yet many acts of innovation require straying from the system or at least testing it.

Committees, but certainly not project teams, are much used by the separated managers. Committees are impersonal and appear to be founded on the rational principle that several heads are better than one. The use of committees leads to orderly changes in power structure, in decision responsibility, and in systems and procedure. Committee members are chosen for the power position they represent rather than for their ability to solve the problem. A deserter (a less effective separated manager) would use committees to induce rigidity rather than order and to diffuse or disguise responsibility rather than to share or concentrate it.

Separated managers believe they owe personal obedience to no one, and no one owes it to them. Authority is impersonal. Obedience is based squarely on established procedures, regulations, and managerial position. Separated managers do not like their decisions to be questioned. They see themselves as autonomous within the sphere of their position description. This helps explain why bureaucrats are sometimes called 'autocrats'. They place the rules so far ahead of the individual that they are sometimes seen as being unnecessarily nasty. Separated managers usually prefer that managerial levels be clearly distinguished by status devices, such as desks, offices, and carpets. To some extent such devices are always present in large organizations, but separated managers can carry them to extremes.

Separated managers want the system to control them. Most children learn, and then accept as their own, social regulations, values and attitudes. By doing this, they know that society then will not hurt them and, in fact, will value their behaviour. Rule following can be likened to a desire to be loved by a powerful yet detached figure. Separated managers usually very much want to become part of the whole. They may want, in effect, to marry the organization. As an extreme, they may be aging bachelors with no life outside the organization, or they may be anyone with little effective involvement with other people who still want to get involved somehow yet on an impersonal basis.

'Identification' is the name given to the process of obtaining personal satisfaction through the existence and activities of something or someone other than oneself. The identification may be with the organization and its rules, superiors, coworkers, or subordinates or the work technology. Separated managers identify with the organization and its rules.

Within fairly narrow limits, we all have to make our peace with the standards that society imposes. Some learn to do this easily in childhood, while others do not. Those who do not may use a great deal of energy in fighting the standards, and those who do, like the separated manager, may embrace the rules and become 'true believers'. This latter form can be a satisfactory adjustment because no longer is society or the organization giving orders to us; instead, we are giving orders to ourselves which can serve to lower the tensions that some feel at being ordered around.

The related style of manager

Related managerial behaviour is characterized by low task orientation and high relationships orientation. It is called related because of its emphasis on relationships with people. The related manager tends to be accepting and friendly and to create a secure atmosphere for others to work in (Exhibit 6.4).

RELATED MANAGER INDICATORS
- People come first
- Emphasizes personal development
- Informal/quiet/unnoticed
- Long conversations
- Sympathetic/accepting/friendly
- Creates secure atmosphere

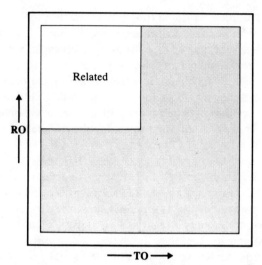

Exhibit 6.4   *The related style. It has a low task orientation and a high relationships orientation*

How related managers differ

Related managers are ones who accept others as they find them. They enjoy long conversations as a way of getting to know others better. Because of this they tend to obtain a lot of useful information from their subordinates. They are not too concerned with time and this in part allows them to get to know others better, particularly subordinates with whom they identify. They see organizations primarily as social systems and judge their subordinates on how well they understand others. They judge superiors on the warmth they show to subordinates. In committees they support others, harmonize differences, and coach others to give their best. They are particularly suited for managing professional workers, for some kinds of training and development work, and for co-ordinating positions where the low power of the position tends to demand a related style if effectiveness is to be achieved. They find it very unpleasant to work with little contact with others. If they find themselves in such a job, they may redesign it so that they can have high contact even though this could lead to decreased overall effectiveness. Their subordinates co-operate well with each other partly because of their examples and partly because they tend to pass over errors and smother conflict with pleasantness. When facing stress they tend to become dependent on others and depressed. Their positive source of influence is likely to be praise while their negative source of influence tends to be the rejection of the individual as a worthy person. While their subordinates like working for related managers, the characteristic problem they encounter is lack of direction from them. The punishment most often used is loss of interest in subordinates. While they value people highly they tend to undervalue the importance of the organization and its technology. One of their weaknesses is sentimentality and a personal fear is one of being rejected by others. The thing they most fear in others is conflict.

Related managers are basically oriented to other people. Effective managers with a related basic style are often found in personnel, training, research management, and sometimes in managing large clerical offices. They may sometimes be the top person in a division or company paired with a key immediate subordinate with a dedicated style.

Related managers can produce a work atmosphere of security and acceptance. Subordinates will then feel free to contribute in every way they can or think they can. They will be willing to participate in a variety of tasks, even those which do not directly affect them. In a flexible, loose structure, where subordinates know more about some things than their superior, this style can lead to effectiveness. In a formal, continuous-flow production process it may not.

Related managers identify with their subordinates and through them fulfil their own needs. The process is much the same as the way in which college students identify with their football team and parents with their children. This identification can centre on the subordinates' growth, hence leading to the developer style, or on the subordinates' personal needs, hence leading to the missionary style.

Subordinates are usually attracted to the related manager. As in the family situation, they represent a needed source of support and affection. However, the rivalry over who should get this attention can create problems. The little direction they offer leaves much unsaid. This ambiguity may create tension, or it may lead to the solution of otherwise difficult problems.

Related managers use friendship and understanding to influence others. They are reluctant to use their authority, and prefer to see good points. Related managers are usually aware of their own attitudes and assumptions about themselves, other individuals, and groups. They know when to look inward to find an explanation or solution rather than outward. By being open to this kind of enquiry, they are careful listeners to the views of others. In addition, they are skilful in making their point of view and feelings known.

Related managers are more sensitive to the demands of the human system than the demands of the technical system. As long as directions are not needed and personal subordinate involvement is essential, the style can be an effective one.

An interest in participative management does not necessarily indicate a related style. Some managers use so-called 'related techniques' to bypass people who should be in on the decision making, but with whom they disagree. Superiors may suggest, for instance, that participation be applied two levels down. They thus could manipulate the intermediate level out of its legitimate part in the decision making process. High sounding labels may be given to such schemes, such as 'democratic leadership', but it may be manipulation just the same.

The dedicated style of manager

Managerial behaviour characterized by high task orientation but low relationships orientation is designated dedicated because of its emphasis on task completion. The dedicated manager tends to be hardworking, aggressive and independent (Exhibit 6.5).

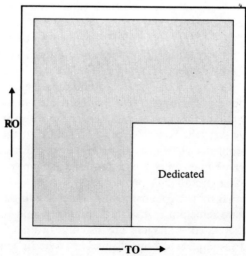

Exhibit 6.5   *The dedicated style. It has a high task orientation and a low relationships orientation*

DEDICATED MANAGER INDICATORS
- Determined/aggressive/confident
- Busy/driving/initiating
- Sets individual tasks and standards
- Self-reliant/independent/ambitious
- Uses rewards, punishments, controls
- Tasks come first

How dedicated managers differ

Dedicated managers tend to dominate others. They give many verbal directions to subordinates. Their time perspective is immediate so when they have the choice they prefer to 'do it now'. They identify with superiors and with the technical system of the firm. When possible they emphasize the demands of the technological rather than the human system. They judge subordinates on the degree to which they produce and superiors on their skill in using power. They play a very active part in committees and initiate, evaluate, and direct a great deal. They are well suited for some kinds of production management where directions are needed, and also for sales management. They do not work too well in situations where they have only a little power because they then cannot easily tell people what to do. Their subordinates soon learn that performance is the thing that counts and punishment can be expected if they are in error. They deal with conflict by suppressing it and deal with other stressful situations by domination. They believe that rewards are a good way to influence others or to be influenced themselves. And they also believe that punishments are the best way to stop people from doing things they should not, and the most severe punishment is loss of position. Their subordinates often complain about lack of information. Dedicated managers tend to forget that they exist as independent entities and do not give enough value to their individual expectations. Their main weakness is that they argue with others when matters could be solved another way. They emphasize the use of power so much that the loss of it is what they fear most. Their biggest fear about others is that they will not produce.

Dedicated managers are likely to cast up grand programmes by themselves and then spend time reshaping the organization to see that the programmes are followed. They show that they mean business, and the implicit message they send to subordinates is either get on or get off. If their subordinates are highly mobile, as are many professional workers, they are likely to leave them. Partly because of this easy mobility, the dedicated style is often inappropriate with professional workers.

Dedicated managers prefer one-to-one management decision making. They deal with subordinates as individuals and make each directly accountable to them for a specific set of responsibilities. There is seldom the problem of overlapping of responsibilities, but lack of work integration can occur.

The dedicated style may or may not lead to sound management development. Its effectiveness in development depends on the time length of the control loop. Dedicated managers who check daily on subordinate performance and correct it may inhibit rather than foster development. Managers, with still the same emphasis on performance, who check monthly will get better results. It is becoming clear that a superb management-development device for new managers is to give them a series of difficult jobs with tough objectives associated with each. The dedicated idea of 'perform or else' is still clearly present, but the manager is not actually breathing down a subordinate's neck.

Dedicated managers prefer to influence their subordinates through their own dedication to hard work. They prefer to motivate by various types of incentive plans based on quantity or quality. They know the workings and limits of the firm's reward-and-punishment system, and they use it.

Dedicated technology

Work technology may demand the use of the dedicated style. Time pressures may be high, emergencies may often arise, the work may be dangerous or intrinsically uninteresting, group problem solving may be unimportant, and quality and quantity may be easily measurable. Even if the technology does not demand dedicated behaviour, the manager who is characteristically dedicated identifies with and is heavily influenced by it, rather than by any other situational element.

Dedicated managers know a great deal about their jobs. They have to, or they cannot operate in the style they have chosen. In relying less on subordinates for information, they must rely more on themselves. They alone tend to define the problem and the route to solutions. This style, then, is often used effectively when there is a wide experience range between levels.

There is much confusion over the potential effectiveness of the dedicated style. A large number of management writers, suggesting that it is generally less effective, call the style 'autocrat' and leave it at that. Yet most managers know that it is this style which is often the most effective, in both the short and long run, within their own company.

People who drive themselves but do not drive others cannot be called 'dedicated' managers. Managing involves others, and one's orientation with respect to them is the important consideration. Managers who work ten hours a day in their office and ignore their subordinates obviously work hard, but, as managers, they may be deserters or bureaucrats. If they are scientists or other essentially solitary workers whose positions require them to work alone, they also may be bureaucrats.

Dedicated managers are most useful when much must be done very quickly or when a profound change of any kind is needed. If a firm hand and clear directions are essential, virtually all other basic styles will lead to less effectiveness. Dedicated managers seldom flounder. They make decisions quickly. They have a single direction which they maintain. Not all will agree on the direction, but it will be established clearly.

The dedicated organization

Some types of organization philosophy may be characterized as dedicated and thus support the use of the dedicated style even in some positions where, in other firms, another style might be appropriate. This type of organization is not too difficult to identify: the top manager is often dedicated; managers most likely to be promoted are dedicated; the general orientation is task first and people second.

The dedicated style is very likely to be effective if most managers in a company use it. This structures the expectations of all subordinates towards it and thus increases their acceptance of it.

Dedicated subordinates

Under some conditions, the nature of the subordinates themselves will suggest the use of the dedicated style. They may simply expect to be managed that way because of either prior experience or training. The subordinates may lack decision skills or be quite willing to obey, may fear punishment or overvalue rewards, and may lack knowledge or be simply insecure.

The dedicated style is appealing to those subordinates who are not frightened by it and who also agree on the direction taken. It is disliked intensely by separated subordinates who prefer to be left alone or by those who have their own independent ideas on policy. The style is more effective in crisis situations and less effective in administration, research, or educational settings, except by top managers. Many good college presidents, especially those facilitating and managing change, are seen as autocrats, yet any objective appraisal would suggest benevolent autocrat or even executive as closer to the truth. These last two are two of the more effective styles that are defined in Exhibit 6.11.

The integrated style of manager

Managerial behaviour characterized by both high task and high relationships orientation is called integrated because it combines both orientations. The integrated manager prefers shared objectives—teamwork (Exhibit 6.6).

INTEGRATED MANAGER INDICATORS
- Derives authority from aims and ideals
- Integrates individual with organization
- Wants participation

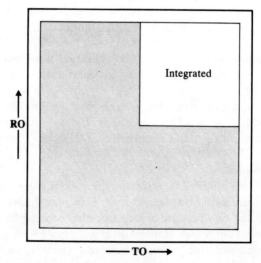

Exhibit 6.6 *The integrated style. It has a high task orientation and a high relationships orientation*

- Prefers shared objectives
- Interested in motivational techniques
- Prefers teamwork

How integrated managers differ

Integrated managers like to become part of things. They are essentially joiners and they take great pains in getting appropriately involved with individuals or groups over work. They like to communicate with others in group settings and use meetings frequently. Through them they can obtain the two-way communication they prefer. Their orientation is always to the future. Because they have no real concern for power differentials they identify strongly with coworkers and emphasize teamwork. They use teamwork and other methods to integrate individual needs with technological needs. They naturally judge subordinates on their willingness to join the team. They judge their superiors on their skill in teamwork. In committee activities they tend to be active in setting team performance standards, testing the team members for their commitment and purpose, and motivating them. The work they are most suited for is the manager of interacting managers. The work they are least suited for is that with a high component of routine. Their employees are usually fully committed and involved, and this is facilitated in part by their intention of learning from errors rather than punishing them. They are interested in investigating the cause of conflict rather than avoiding, smothering, or suppressing it. In highly stressful situations they tend to postpone making decisions. They tend to control others by proposing common ideals or settling for a compromise. Because of this integrated style and emphasis on the group, their subordinates often feel a lack of independence. Because of their use of ideals to motivate, the punishment they can best use involves loss of self-respect in the person punished. They sometimes undervalue the need for independent action and sometimes use participation inappropriately. Their greatest fear about themselves is that they might become uninvolved. Their greatest fear about others is that they might become dissatisfied.

Integrated managers always use both task and relationships orientation. Almost all such behaviour involves either motivational techniques or the setting of overall aims and ideals. Effective managers who are integrated are often found supervising other managers who have to interact in making decisions. Integrated managers wish to structure things so there are highly co-operative approaches toward the achievement of organization goals. They develop skills in what are essentially personal motivational techniques. They use a maximum task orientation and relationships orientation to produce effectiveness. Integrated managers use a variety of participative techniques. Through them they attempt to flatten their power differential with respect to subordinates, make their authority less personal, and obtain their subordinates' commitment to decisions and changes.

Integrated managers go to some lengths to make sure their subordinates understand why they are being asked to do something. This will usually go quite beyond advising them of a reason for a change—an act which even dedicated managers might do. Integrated managers want them to accept the reasons for change and will use a variety of devices to facilitate such acceptance. Clearly, this approach might be very appropriate for a senior manager but considerably less appropriate for a supervisor, especially if faced with union militancy.

Integrated managers want to depersonalize authority. To be successful at this they must substitute ideals, aims, goals, or policies, in the name of which certain responses are expected. This ideal may be simply 'for the good of the firm', Theory Y or 9.9. If subordinates can be taught to respond appropriately to one or another of these then they may be used as impersonal control devices. Although few would salute two flags, many are prepared to die for one.

Clearly the integrated approach is based on the idea that subordinates must be 'turned on' in order for effectiveness to be achieved. Its use suggests that unless certain ideals or end results are jointly accepted, subordinates will not put forth their best efforts.

Integrated managers want to integrate the needs of the individual with the needs of the organization. They want to align personal goals with organization goals. To do this requires a sound understanding of the subordinate as an individual and, usually, a longer time period over which changes are to be made. Clearly a blanket use of this style is based on an idealistic view of all situations and people in all organizations.

Misunderstandings of the integrated style
One problem in being objective about the integrated style is that many managers see themselves as integrated when in fact they are not. There is little doubt that the integrated style is an attractive one and is often appropriate. But there is also little doubt that its very

attractiveness may lead to its being used in situations where it is inappropriate.

Those who persistently misuse the integrated style usually have serious distortions of the nature of human motivation or simply do not understand the superior–subordinate contract. In its simplest form the contract is pay in return for obedience and effort. This is honourable enough, although many managers feel guilty about it and thus overuse various motivational or participative techniques.

Some managers claim that the integrated style is a 'fuzzy beast', that they do not understand it, and that they have no idea of how to use it. They ask how a manager can use high TO and RO at the same time. Those who ask this question are very often those who currently encounter a situation in which it cannot be used but, perhaps, have been told in the past they should use it. Not knowing what the style really is may simply mean that in their career so far, the manager has not encountered a situation where it is clearly appropriate.

This integrated style is close to the ideal management style proposed by several university professors: McGregor's Theory Y, Likert's System 4, and Blake's 9.9.

But what about effectiveness?

It is absolutely essential for every manager to come to grips with the possibility that any basic style may be effective at times. Many traditional approaches to style do not claim this. If one accepts the position that any basic style may be effective at times then further information is needed. This information includes:

- A clear definition of effectiveness
- A clear description of the four basic styles in their more effective and less effective use
- Some guidelines as to when each of the four basic styles would probably lead to a more effective outcome

All this leads directly to the need for an introduction of a third dimension in addition to task and relationships. This third dimension is obviously effectiveness. Effectiveness is defined as the extent to which a manager achieves the output requirements of the position. For some positions and some situations the need may be for separated behaviour and for others it may be any of the other three basic styles. It is only by measuring effectiveness that one can determine whether a basic style is being used appropriately or not.

There is a great deal of research to make it fairly obvious that there is no ideal style. The style must suit the situation, therefore styles must be varied and style flexibility must be the key. Styles either suit situations or they do not suit situations. Styles then are embedded in situations where they are appropriate or embedded in situations where they are inappropriate.

The front of Exhibit 6.7 is the plane of the four less effective styles, the middle is the four basic styles plane and the back is the plane of more effectiveness. There are thus eight styles, which include all possible combinations of high and low on task and relationships and effectiveness, and are called the eight managerial styles of the 3-D theory.

Exhibit 6.7 has introduced a third dimension, in addition to task orientation and relationships orientation. This third dimension, obviously, is effectiveness. This exhibit shows another way of linking effectiveness, situation and style. The idea being conveyed is that the dedicated style may be used where it is inappropriate, in which case it is called autocrat or the dedicated style may be used in a situation

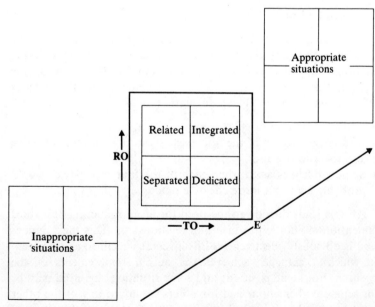

Exhibit 6.7   *Styles are embedded in situations. Basic styles are used in situations which are inappropriate or appropriate to them*

where it is appropriate and in this case it is called benevolent autocrat. The use of the dedicated style to ask your secretary for a cup of coffee is usually inappropriate and can be seen as autocratic. To use the dedicated style to shout, 'Fire, everyone get out!' would be seen as appropriate and the term 'autocratic' would hardly apply.

Eight style labels have been developed, each the subject of one of our next eight chapters, to describe the four basic styles used in situations where they are inappropriate and in situations where they are appropriate. Exhibit 6.8 adds the eight labels.

These styles are called managerial styles to differentiate them from the four basic styles. Basic styles deal with types of behaviour with no comment on whether the behaviour is effective or not. The eight managerial styles deal with behaviour, situation, and the level of effectiveness indicating whether the style suits the situation or not.

Let us look at Exhibit 6.8 in detail. The separated style when used inappropriately is labelled deserter. When used appropriately, mainly by managers concerned with system maintenance, the term bureaucrat is used.

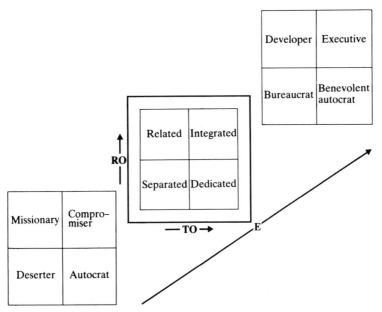

Exhibit 6.8   *The 3-D style model. The complete 3-D style model consists of four basic styles, four more effective managerial styles and four less effective managerial styles*

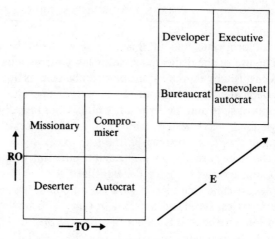

Exhibit 6.9 *The 3-D managerial style model. The middle plane may be omitted once the basic style concept is understood*

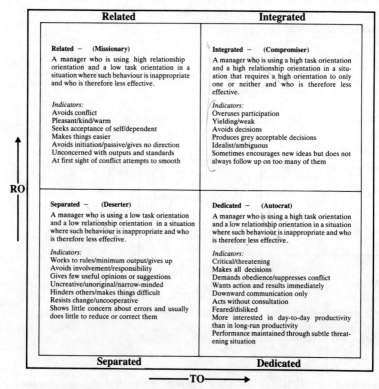

Related	Integrated
Related — (Missionary) A manager who is using high relationship orientation and a low task orientation in a situation where such behaviour is inappropriate and who is therefore less effective. *Indicators:* Avoids conflict Pleasant/kind/warm Seeks acceptance of self/dependent Makes things easier Avoids initiation/passive/gives no direction Unconcerned with outputs and standards At first sight of conflict attempts to smooth	**Integrated — (Compromiser)** A manager who is using a high task orientation and a high relationship orientation in a situation that requires a high orientation to only one or neither and who is therefore less effective. *Indicators:* Overuses participation Yielding/weak Avoids decisions Produces grey acceptable decisions Idealist/ambiguous Sometimes encourages new ideas but does not always follow up on too many of them
Separated — (Deserter) A manager who is using a low task orientation and a low relationship orientation in a situation where such behaviour is inappropriate and who is therefore less effective. *Indicators:* Works to rules/minimum output/gives up Avoids involvement/responsibility Gives few useful opinions or suggestions Uncreative/unoriginal/narrow-minded Hinders others/makes things difficult Resists change/uncooperative Shows little concern about errors and usually does little to reduce or correct them	**Dedicated — (Autocrat)** A manager who is using a high task orientation and a low relationship orientation in a situation where such behaviour is inappropriate and who is therefore less effective. *Indicators:* Critical/threatening Makes all decisions Demands obedience/suppresses conflict Wants action and results immediately Downward communication only Acts without consultation Feared/disliked More interested in day-to-day productivity than in long-run productivity Performance maintained through subtle threatening situation
Separated	**Dedicated**

Exhibit 6.10 *Four basic styles when used inappropriately*

The related style when used inappropriately is called missionary. The related style when used appropriately because the object is developing people rather than simply being nice to them is called developer.

The dedicated style when used inappropriately is called autocrat and when used appropriately it is called benevolent autocrat.

The integrated style when used inappropriately is called compromiser and when used appropriately is called executive.

Exhibit 6.9 is the usual way of showing the eight styles alone.

Exhibits 6.10 and 6.11 contain the definitions and indicators in detail.

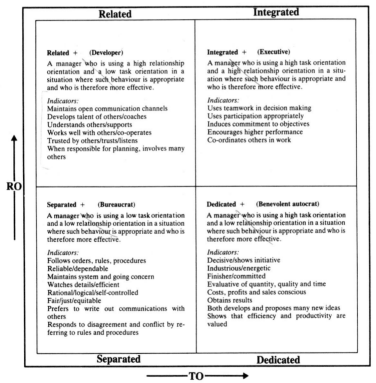

Exhibit 6.11   *Four basic styles when used appropriately*

PART 3

Your eight managerial styles

This part exclusively concerns managerial style. From it you will gain a much greater understanding of the eight managerial styles of the 3-D theory. There is a chapter on each of the eight styles. Using the test you completed in Chapter 3 you will obtain a good idea of how you scored on each of the styles.

If your adjusted score for each managerial style is four or less, it is over-reject, ten is supporting and eleven or more is dominant.

7. Are you a deserter?

Managers don't come to organizations as deserters, they are driven to it.

Deserter managers really enjoy work; they can sit and watch it for hours.

The deserter manager (Exhibit 7.1) is one who is using a low task' orientation and a low relationships orientation in a situation where such behaviour is inappropriate and who is therefore less effective.

Exhibit 7.1   *The deserter*

Deserter indicators

- Works to rules/minimum output/gives up
- Avoids involvement and responsibility
- Gives few useful opinions or suggestions
- Uncreative/unoriginal/narrow-minded
- Hinders others/makes things difficult
- Resists change/uncooperative
- Shows little concern about errors and usually does little to correct or reduce them

Some things the deserter might say include:

'The boss is asking about that report and is getting hot about it. I don't know why—it's not that important.'
'If you don't understand it, forget it.'

'If at first you don't succeed, give up.'

'I love my job; it's the work I hate.'

'Mistakes are bound to happen, particularly when I give them a little help.'

'Think—there must be a harder way to do the job.'

'Let's send the whole thing back to a committee.'

'I really cannot give an opinion on that.'

'I really enjoy work. I can sit and watch it for hours.'

'There is just no reason for it—it's just some company policy.'

'I don't know and I don't care.'

Some things others might say about deserters include:

'They have a great labour saving device—tomorrow.'

'They've stopped drinking tea or coffee in the morning because it keeps them awake the rest of the day.'

Deserter behaviour and effects

Deserters can be seen as scar tissue on the organization. They may have been kicked upstairs, kicked downstairs, ignored or badly treated and now they want to get their own back. The main emphasis for deserters is survival. They may watch hungrily for the clock to approach five, so that they can get out of work immediately. They do not want to make any waves and will usually agree to anything.

Deserter managers are essentially separated managers in the wrong situation. They are seen as the ones who often show their lack of interest in both task and relationships. They are less effective not only because of their lack of interest but also because of their effect on morale. They may be seen not only as shirking their own duties but also as hindering the performance of others through intervention or by withholding information.

In its refined form and in modern organizations, desertion is likely to reveal itself in resistance to change or in accepting change and then quietly sabotaging it; making all things difficult, withholding information up or down, aiming for minimum output, impeding others, and lowering morale—deserter managers use the whole range. Desertion is to be found more often in the large than in the small company. It is more easily hidden.

Organization life can be seen as a game, and as in games, people sometimes get hurt. Some are hurt deliberately and some accidentally; sometimes no one else knows it; sometimes the hurt is imaginary. Deserter managers often feel they have been hurt and have never got over it. This may be a result of change that was clumsily introduced. Whether they have been kicked aside, kicked downstairs, or just ignored, no matter what the case, the important thing is that they think they have been treated unfairly. They have decided that they will try to ignore the demands of the organization as much as possible. Their avoidance of task and relationships is often handled in highly sophisticated ways so that only close observation will disclose it.

Deserters are more to be pitied than anything else because they have usually been made deserters by a major management error. People do not come to organizations acting this way. They are driven to it. The issue for managers is not only how to change the style of deserters but also to prevent more deserters being created.

Deserter behaviour is often a general example of displaced aggression which is turned towards an essentially innocent party. In its simplest form, it shows itself in the managers who would like to have a shouting match with their superiors but instead have one with subordinates. This unjustified attack is certainly being nasty, but it is not autocracy since no task orientation is involved. It is best called desertion. Aggression may be turned toward oneself so that the person may become accident-prone in the physical or administrative sense.

Such displacement helps the managers using it but seldom helps the organization. It is of considerable value to managers because it enables them to express aggression without incurring retaliation from the individuals they really fear. Displacement is essentially desertion because the real problem is not faced. In addition, the displacement may become so deviant that the deserter's action leads to direct harm to the organization.

The deserter managers aim for output just high enough to keep people from bothering them. They may remain uninvolved by pleading insufficient information. They follow up very slowly, like to send things to committees in order to bury them, and want minimum involvement. They develop a wondrous array of techniques to accomplish this. As they do not do too much anyway, and often enjoy their desertion, they have the time and inclination to invent creative ways to inhibit change.

Deserter managers are skilled at avoiding responsibility. They know how to use separated techniques as tools to slow things down, sometimes to a halt. They will use the letter rather than the spirit of the regulations. Often they will point to the rules to prove they cannot make a decision. They know how to use the system to pass the buck and to avoid sticking their necks out. They limit their discretionary powers to a vanishing point. Those subjected to their behaviour call it 'red tape'.

Deserters may ask whether the approval to initiate the task has been fully cleared. They may ask whether the project is fully defined. If they think they are in a strong enough position, they will simply turn it down, perhaps on the grounds that it is against their principles or simply is not their job. They may do all this in a forthright and even aggressive way to mask their underlying desertion.

If a decision is likely to be a particularly sticky or complex one, deserter managers will postpone action on it. At the extreme this may take the ostrich approach of head in the sand—believing that to ignore a problem is likely to send it away. More often their action will be to pass the file to others, pigeonhole it, or raise complex procedural questions concerning it. By these devices the deserter buys time but may pay for it with interest when the decision has to be confronted. Small problems when delayed sometimes go away; they also sometimes magnify.

Separated managers can easily revert to desertion by using the organization's rules against itself. A popular worker parallel to this form of sabotage is the 'work-to-rule' strategy. By following all procedures to the letter, slowdowns inevitably result; managers sometimes have sophisticated 'work-to-rule' programmes of their own. They may be ingenious and disguised, but the effects are the same.

Deserters have the amazing ability to act as computers at the most inopportune time. They can rattle off detailed facts and arguments to prove that a particular plan is unworkable. They know all the reasons why things cannot be done. This may often be facilitated by a high verbal fluency and an intellectual camouflage. Deserters who can use statistics well are often hard to spot for what they are and sometimes hard to stop.

If inappropriate deserter behaviour is prolonged, managers can actually come to find it satisfying to obstruct and resist others. They may be quite willing to endure discomfort themselves for the pleasure of maintaining their negative stand. A very clear example of this is the people who pursue a course of action knowing that it will eventually lead to their exclusion from the group or the company. To maintain this immature behaviour, a facesaving device is essential. It is usually some principle, some rule, or some set of procedures which deserters claim are inviolate.

Deserter managers can make deserters of their subordinates. Less experienced subordinates may be led to believe that desertion is a reasonable response to the organization so long as they do not get caught. Others may move to desertion in disgust at their superiors' behaviour and in their knowledge that they may have no power to change the situation. There is usually no incentive to work effectively for a deserter superior because the rewards and recognition may be low or even in the wrong direction.

Deserter managers generally prefer to avoid loose, open, un-structured personal conflict so, instead, use the files or rules as weapons. These may be used to attack just as surely as the sword. They usually like to keep a copy of every memo they send and use them as 'alibi papers' to prove they took action. Deserters will often resist, inhibit, or even prevent major change by using outdated but unreplaced rules.

Some deserters are ambitious, and in a company with poor managerial measurement devices they may well advance. Many problems can be avoided for years, such as the low-performing subordinate, the major restructuring of a policy or procedure, the extensive survey of markets, customers, or technologies, and the provision for management succession. Deserters may lead quiet, cordial lives putting off all these problems for their successors. They keep the lid on until they have gone. The crisis is their successor's problem, not their own. Incompetent senior management may not spot this desertion for years and may think the successors are incompetent because they seem to have so many new problems with which to deal.

Ambitious deserter managers can exist in an organization with poor control techniques and a poor reward-and-punishment system. These managers usually develop skills in personal effectiveness and apparent effectiveness but are not directly concerned with their managerial effectiveness.

Deserters may become so concerned over status rather than managerial effectiveness that they become empire builders. They are interested in increasing their personal effectivenesss by enlarging their apparent importance. They will spend an inordinate amount of time in scheming to obtain more subordinates, more space, and more power. All this may have no real relationship to the actual demands of the position. They are interested in makework projects which will add subordinates, more or less permanently.

Some forms of desertion are founded in avoidance behaviour designed to protect the manager from threatening situations. Some deserters are simply scared. They say, 'No!' or are stubborn because to do otherwise might expose them, they believe, to situations difficult to face.

Some emotionally immature managers resort to what is essentially childish behaviour in an attempt to solve their adult problems. Their behaviour might be the equivalent of a temper tantrum or sulking. The psychologists call this 'regression'. The particular form it takes depends on what behaviour was successful for the manager during early development. Normal amounts of regression are apparent when people revert to adolescent behaviour at conventions and reunions. Abnormal amounts lead to desertion.

These managers have not had an opportunity to grow up. Like spoiled children who find things different at boarding school, deserters decide to withdraw and so inhibit the development of their own social maturity. In boarding schools, as in organizations, we see those who have psychologically fled from their surroundings. They are quiet, friendless, unnoticed, little respected. The rituals of the institution carry them on, beginning with the 8.00 a.m. chapel or the opening of the mail, but they might as well not be there.

Do deserters come to an organization acting that way? Very few come to organizations planning to act as deserters; most are driven to it. It is better to ask, 'How do we avoid creating more?' than, 'How can we get rid of them?' The main way to do it is change their situation.

In a study of 970 managers, we looked at whether any of the eight styles occurred at particular levels in an organization hierarchy. There was no differentiation in the number of deserters at the various levels. They exist at all levels. They are the people marking time until retirement. Some start young.

Your deserter score and how to change it

Your score

Turn back to Exhibit 3.1 to obtain your adjusted scores on the deserter scale. It is the last line under A. If your score is 11 or above, it indicates that you have a dominant style of deserter. That is, it is a style you use frequently. If your score is 10 you have a supporting style of deserter. That is, a style you resort to fairly frequently. If your score is four or below you are over-rejecting the deserter style, that is, you use it very little if at all.

At this point only one style is being considered. After you have looked at each of your eight styles individually the styles will be looked at together as a style profile.

It is important to remind you that this test measures your behaviour in the job you now have. If your score is high on this style it is not indicative that you are like it permanently. This is not a test of personality, it is a test of your behaviour in the job you now have.

Changing your behaviour
The statements below reflect deserter behaviour. As you see, they reflect deserter behaviour with all of the 20 situational elements in Exhibit 5.3. Should you wish to decrease your deserter score then change your behaviour with respect to one or more of these.

1. *Superior*
   I do not show too much interest in maintaining good relation-ships with those above me.

2. *Coworkers*
   I do not give as much priority as I should in maintaining good relationships with other departments.

3. *Subordinates*
   I do not show too much interest in my subordinates.

4. *Staff advisers*
   I feel it is not usually worth the effort to cooperate with staff advisers.

5. *Unions*
   I have little sympathy or interest in unions and what they stand for.

6. *Customers*
   I have little interest in myself or others maintaining sound relationships with the customers.

7. *General public*
I believe the company should have little or no concern with the interests of the general public.

8. *Creativity*
I believe the value of creativity, change and innovation is often overemphasized.

9. *Objectives*
I think that the idea of setting overall objectives can be overdone.

10. *Planning*
I think that planning is not really as important as some people think.

11. *Change introduction*
I think that the actual introduction of a change requires little effort on my part.

12. *Implementation*
I am not too interested in the actual implementation of decisions.

13. *Controls*
I am not too interested in control procedures.

14. *Evaluation*
I believe that evaluation and review are often overstressed.

15. *Productivity*
I am not too interested in improving productivity just for its own sake.

16. *Communication*
I could supply much more useful information to others than I do.

17. *Conflict*
I avoid conflict even when facing it would be useful.

18. *Errors*
    I show little concern about errors and usually do little to correct or reduce them.

19. *Meetings*
    I do not seem interested in meetings even when they might be useful.

20. *Teamwork*
    I have no opinion one way or the other about the team approach to management.

8. Are you a missionary?

Some managers have no philosophy and their style is essentially that of the bland leading the bland.

The missionary manager (Exhibit 8.1) is one who is using high relationships orientation and low task orientation in a situation where such behaviour is inappropriate and who is therefore less effective.

Exhibit 8.1   *The missionary*

Missionary indicators

- Avoids conflict
- Pleasant/kind/warm
- Seeks acceptance of self/dependent
- Makes things easier
- Avoids initiation/passive/gives no direction
- Unconcerned with outputs and standards
- At first sign of conflict attempts to smooth

Some things the missionary might say include:

> 'The boss is asking about that report. I hope that it won't inconvenience you to let me know how it is coming when you have the time.'
>
> 'Fringe benefits should always be increased rather than profits.'

'Look after the people and the organization will look after itself.'

'Argument and conflict never solved anything.'

'The best company is a harmonious company.'

'Harmony leads directly to higher morale and productivity.'

'Conflict is a negative human quality.'

'Day by day, in every way, people are getting better and better.'

'I changed my mind to minimize the chance that someone might be hurt.'

'Keep people happy and they will look after the rest.'

Some things others might say about missionaries include:

'Their remarks are always more candied than candid.'

'They like to do things the herd way, not the hard way.'

'They treat subordinates with great kindness and consideration.'

'They allow subordinates to set their own objectives according to their needs and accept them even if somewhat unsatisfactory.'

'They believe that if an error occurs it should be corrected in such a way that no one will be upset.'

Missionary behaviour and effects

Missionary managers are ones using the related style in a situation in which it is inappropriate. Missionary managers are basically kindly souls who put happy relationships above all other considerations. They are ineffective because their desire to see themselves and be seen as 'good people' prevent them from risking even mild disagreement in order to improve production.

Missionary managers believe that happy people produce more. They attempt to run their departments like a social club because they believe that production is less important than good fellowship. They strive to create a warm, pleasant, social atmosphere where an easygoing work tempo may be maintained. Kind and pleasant to everyone, they never want to rock the boat for fear that someone may get upset.

Missionary managers spend much of their time trying to find ways to make things easier for their people. If you want one person, they will give you two; if you want to exceed their budget, they will immediately consent. Their attitude toward conflict leads to poor management and low output. They think that conflict is out of place in an organization, that no good ideas are developed by an argument, and that mature people never argue. When conflict arises, they smother it with concern for the feelings involved. They deal with hot issues by waiting for them to cool down. They are masters at pouring oil on troubled waters and so avoid dealing with the problems beneath.

The missionaries' management style is less effective because they always put human problems first in situations where they may not really demand priority. They avoid those who argue and prefer that difficult human problems be solved by transfer, promotion, or pay rises.

They naturally discuss all issues. They are willing to change their mind to keep the peace. What is worse, they think this is always the best thing to do.

Missionary managers carry identification with others too far and for the wrong reasons. They may identify so strongly with their subordinates and their personal needs that they essentially join them. They give up their roles as managers.

The main thing to know about the missionary is that when they smile at you, they are not saying, 'I like you': they are saying, 'I want you to like me'. It is dependent behaviour. Missionaries are easy to get on with. They are driven by, rather than driving, the situation. They are serving their own needs, as are all the less effective styles.

Your missionary score and how to change it

Your score
Turn back to Exhibit 3.1 to obtain your adjusted score on the missionary scale. It is the last line under B. If your score is 11 or above, it indicates that you have a dominant style of missionary. That is, it is a style you use frequently. If your score is 10 you have a supporting style of missionary. That is, a style you resort to fairly frequently. If your score is four or below you are over-rejecting the missionary style, that is, you use it very little if at all.

At this point only one style is being considered. After you have looked at each of your eight styles individually the styles will be looked at together as a style profile.

It is important to remind you, again, that this test measures your behaviour in the job you now have. If your score is high on this style it is not indicative that you are like it permanently. This is not a test of personality, it is a test of your behaviour in the job you now have.

Changing your behaviour

The statements below reflect missionary behaviour. As you see, they reflect missionary behaviour with all of the twenty situational elements described in Exhibit 5.3. Should you wish to decrease your missionary score then change your behaviour with respect to one or more of these.

1. *Superior*
   I try to avoid disagreements with higher management even though this may lower my own or my subordinates' productivity.

2. *Coworkers*
   I prefer to co-operate and thus avoid any disagreement with other departments.

3. *Subordinates*
   I treat subordinates with great kindness and consideration.

4. *Staff advisers*
   I go out of my way to co-operate with staff advisers. I want to make them feel that they are needed.

5. *Unions*
   I go out of my way to co-operate with union representatives and to keep them as happy as possible.

6. *Customers*
   I believe in maintaining good customer relationships even at high cost to the company.

7. *General public*
   I believe that the general public must be kept content at all times even though productivity might fall.

8. *Creativity*
   I think that many new ideas lead to unnecessary disagreement and friction.

9. *Objectives*
   I allow subordinates to set their own objectives according to their needs and accept them even if they are somewhat unsatisfactory.

10. *Planning*
    I prefer to let individuals set their own plans as long as they do not interfere with the plans of others.

11. *Change introduction*
    I try to introduce changes very gradually so no one will become upset.

12. *Implementation*
    I tolerate deviations in implementing plans if this will avert unpleasantness.

13. *Controls*
    I overlook violations of any kind if it helps to make things run more smoothly.

14. *Evaluation*
    I usually say that a good job has been done whether or not it was really satisfactory.

15. *Productivity*
    I believe the proper treatment of people is more important than productivity.

16. *Communication*
    I communicate with others so as to maintain good relationships above all else.

17. *Conflict*
    At the first sign of conflict I attempt to smooth things over.

18. *Errors*
    I believe that if an error occurs it should be corrected in such a way that no one will be upset.

19. *Meetings*
    I like meetings to run harmoniously.

20. *Teamwork*
    I believe that team meetings are good primarily because they get people to talk together more.

9. Are you an autocrat?

Some managers do not want to be surrounded by those who say 'yes'. When they say 'no', they want the subordinates to say 'no'.

The autocrat believes in clubs for employees but only if kindness fails.

The autocrat manager (Exhibit 9.1) is one who is using a high task orientation and a low relationships orientation in a situation where such behaviour is inappropriate and who is therefore less effective.

Exhibit 9.1   *The autocrat*

Autocrat indicators

- Critical/threatening
- Makes decisions
- Demands obedience/suppresses conflict
- Wants action and results immediately
- Downward communication only
- Acts without consultation
- Feared/disliked
- More interested in day to day productivity than in long run productivity
- Performance maintained through subtle threatening situation

Some things the autocrat might say include:
'The boss is asking about that report, and is hot about it and so am I. Get on the ball and let's get some action here.'
'Stop talking while I am interrupting.'

'Let me have your ideas even if it costs you your job.'
'My mind is made up, don't confuse me with the facts.'
'Let me have your opinion—I haven't had a good argument in days.'
'Be reasonable—do it my way.'
'In case you think this is merely a suggestion, folks, you might bear in mind the source.'
'Don't do as I do, do as I say.'

Some things others might say about the autocrat include:

'The rough exterior covers a heart of flint.'
'Some call them a pain in the neck and some people have an even lower opinion of them.'
'They think they are big shots just because they explode.'

Autocrat behaviour and effects

The autocrat arises when dedicated behaviour is used inappropriately. Autocrat managers are usually perceived as ones who put the immediate task above all other considerations. They are less effective in that they make it obvious that they have no concern for relationships and have little confidence in other people. While many fear them, they also dislike them and are thus motivated to work well only when under direct pressure. Autocrat managers cannot understand why so many people are unco-operative. They do not fully realize that co-operation, to them, means doing it their way.

Autocrat managers are perceived as ones who believe that the average human being prefers to be directed, wishes to avoid responsibility, has relatively little ambition, and wants security above all. Autocrat managers thus do not fully utilize the capabilities of others.

Autocrat managers see workers as extensions of machines. A subordinate's job is to follow orders, nothing more. The job of the boss is to plan in detail every aspect of the subordinate's job. Autocrats do not know what 'motivate' means. Their view of work is simple: some people order and others obey. They think that the best committee is the one-person committee, that people work best alone, and that the job of the manager is to generate fear and immediate action. They provide no way to be imaginative. They do not understand the need for recognition by others.

They handle conflict by suppressing it. If they face disagreement from a subordinate, they make it clear that they see it as a challenge to their authority. They do not forgive easily. Autocrat managers have a powerful effect on the organization and do not know it. They help to produce grapevines, cliques, troublemakers, and deserters. At best, they get blind obedience; at worst, they get desertion. Autocrats believe that threats motivate. They might be the sales managers who say, 'If you get to meet your quota, you get to keep your job.'

Autocrat managers will get work accomplished, of course. The accomplishments, however, will be far short of potential. In addition, this style does not provide for a solid foundation of continued performance, and it certainly provides no lasting satisfaction for subordinates.

Subordinates tend to withdraw from autocrat managers and this can lead to further aggressive behaviour by the autocrat on their part. They want to bridge the gap but have no means for doing so, except by using more controls. Their notion of closeness is agreement on the demands of the technological system, not the human one.

In many ways autocrats are simply not in the picture. They want to use more power than their position has, they are more task oriented than the technology demands, and they are less sensitive to relationships than they should be.

Your autocrat score and how to change it

Your score

Turn back to Exhibit 3.1 to obtain your adjusted score on the autocrat scale. It is the last line under C. If your score is 11 or above, it indicates that you have a dominant style of autocrat. That is, it is a style you use frequently. If your score is 10 you have a supporting style of autocrat. That is, a style you resort to fairly frequently. If your score is four or below you are over-rejecting the autocrat style, that is, you use it very little if at all.

At this point only one style is being considered. After you have looked at each of your eight styles individually the styles will be looked at together as a style profile.

It is important to remind you, yet again, that this test measures your behaviour in the job you now have. If your score is high on this style it is not indicative that you are like it permanently. This is not a test of personality, it is a test of your behaviour in the job you now have.

Changing your behaviour

The statements below reflect autocrat behaviour. As you see, they reflect autocrat behaviour with all of the 20 situational elements described in Exhibit 5.3. Should you wish to decrease your autocrat score then change your behaviour with respect to one or more of these.

1. *Superior*
   I want to do my job with as little interference from those above as possible.

2. *Coworkers*
   I believe in doing my job by myself and prefer little involvement with managers of other departments.

3. *Subordinates*
   I direct the work of my subordinates and discourage deviation from my plans.

4. *Staff advisers*
   I tend to avoid or to argue with staff advisers, thinking they often know little of the practical side of things.

5. *Unions*
   I think that union representatives are a nuisance and I prefer to have little to do with them.

6. *Customers*
   I believe my job is to supply a product and the feelings of customers should have little effect on me or the company policy.

7. *General public*
   I believe that what the general public thinks should not influence the company unduly.

8. *Creativity*
   I think new ideas from below are often less useful than those from above.

9. *Objectives*
   Deviations from the specific objectives I set for others are discouraged.

10. *Planning*
    I see planning as a one person job and do not usually involve others or their ideas.

11. *Change introduction*
    I think the best way to introduce change is to make an announcement and then let people get on with it.

12. *Implementation*
    I watch implementation of plans closely, point out errors and criticize where necessary.

13. *Controls*
    I insist that others follow procedures exactly but sometimes object if I am told to do so.

14. *Evaluation*
    I evaluate individuals personally. I frequently point out their good and bad points and criticize where necessary.

15. *Productivity*
    I seem more interested in day to day productivity than in long run productivity.

16. *Communication*
    I am not always as receptive as I might be when others communicate with me and I am good at 'shooting down' ideas.

17. *Conflict*
    When disagreement arises I take a firm stand.

18. *Errors*
    I believe that when errors occur the person responsible should be reprimanded.

19. *Meetings*
    I tend to be dominant at meetings.

20. *Teamwork*
    I believe in 'one person, one job, well done.'

10. Are you a compromiser?

> There is nothing in the world more pitiable than an irresolute person vacillating between two feelings, who would willingly unite the two, and who does not perceive that nothing can unite them.
>
> *Goethe*

> A compromiser who was asked whether it was difficult to make decisions said, 'Well, yes and no.'

The compromiser manager (Exhibit 10.1) is one who is using a high task orientation and a high relationships orientation in a situation that requires a high orientation to only one or neither and who is therefore less effective.

Exhibit 10.1   *The compromiser*

Compromiser indicators

- Overuses participation
- Yielding/weak
- Avoids decisions
- Produces grey acceptable decisions
- Idealist/ambiguous
- Sometimes encourages new ideas but does not always follow up on too many of them

Some things the compromiser might say include:

'The boss is asking about that report. Are you busy now? Can you try and get something down on paper as soon as you have the time?'

'You can convince some of the people some of the time and that's usually enough to get by with.'

'Any plan is really a "best fit" or simply a balance among the conflicting demands of the organization.'

'I want all my people to think my way but only after they have really understood and accepted it.'

Some things others might say about the compromiser include:

'They are always trying to save both faces.'

'That manager has three hats: one to cover the head, one to toss in the ring, and one to talk through.'

'They're real decisive types, you'll always get a definite maybe.'

Compromiser behaviour and effects

The integrated style, when used less effectively, is known as the compromiser. One of the main things to observe about the compromiser is the degree to which they change their minds. They tend to agree with the last person they see.

Compromiser managers are essentially ones who see advantages in being oriented to both task and relationships but who are in jobs where only one or the other or neither is needed or who are unable or unwilling to integrate these ideas and to make sound decisions. Ambivalence and compromise are seen to be their stock in trade. The strongest influence in their decision making process tends to be the most recent or heaviest pressure. They try to minimize immediate problems rather than maximize long term production.

Compromisers, as the name suggests, never do anything well. They push, but not too hard. Whereas they would not condone very poor performance, they show that they do not expect high performance. Compromiser managers are convinced that optimum production is a dream, think that any plan must be a series of compromises and thus look only for what will work in the short term.

Compromisers sometimes use participative techniques when they are clearly inappropriate. It may be that the decision is already made, that the decision to be made is trite, or that the subordinates are in no mood because of expectations or skill to engage in participation. Under such circumstances, the decision will almost certainly be poorer than the one managers might have made on their own. It is likely to be a compromise decision which resolves nothing.

Compromisers are likely to ask their subordinates to participate in a decision which has only a known single good solution. They may already know of the solution, or skilled staff could have advised them of it if they had been consulted. The solution that comes out of such use of participation may be the same single good solution, in which case the time spent was wasted. Increased motivation could hardly arise unless the subordinates were so dim as not to see that only one solution was possible and that management must or should have known it. If the single good solution is not forthcoming, then a compromise will be produced. This will be some kind of balance between what one or more subordinates need and what the organization needs. This poorer grey decision, to which no one is likely to be truly committed, is a direct result of the inappropriate use of an integrated approach.

Compromiser managers avoid conflict by using participation. With strong subordinates this approach can lead to executive infighting among them so that two distinct antagonistic camps develop.

Compromisers have a devasting effect on subordinates who prefer to work from a clear plan. The compromisers' vacillating approach leads to poor goal setting by subordinates because they have no way of predicting the future course of events.

Good decision making often leads to the production of sets of quite different solutions to problems. Any one set alone can lead to success, whereas a combination of two or more can lead to failure. Compromiser managers, not wanting to make decisions, attempt to satisfy several alternatives at once and become even less effective. As an example, managers are sometimes faced with two different alternative methods of solving a particular problem involving people and the organization. It may be that one method essentially favours the organization and the task side of things, and the other favours people and the relationships side of things. Either could be effective if used alone and would lead to the benevolent autocrat or developer style. Compromiser managers, however, would attempt to satisfy both alternative solutions rather than one or the other.

Your compromiser score and how to change it

Your score

Turn back to Exhibit 3.1 to obtain your adjusted score on the compromiser scale. It is the last line under D. If your score is 11 or above, it indicates that you have a dominant style of compromiser. That is, it is a style you use frequently. If your score is 10 you have a supporting style of compromiser. That is, a style you resort to fairly frequently. If your score is four or below you are over-rejecting the compromiser style, that is, you use it very little if at all.

At this point only one style is being considered. After you have looked at each of your eight styles individually the styles will be looked at together as a style profile.

It is important to remind you, yet again, that this test measures your behaviour in the job you now have. If your score is high on this style it is not indicative that you are like it permanently. This is not a test of personality, it is a test of your behaviour in the job you now have.

Changing your behaviour

The statements below reflect compromiser behaviour. As you see they reflect compromiser behaviour with all of the twenty situational elements described in Exhibit 5.3. Should you wish to decrease your compromiser score then change your behaviour with respect to one or more of these.

1. *Superior*
   I want to improve my relationships with my superior but do not always take the action necessary.

2. *Coworkers*
   I want to co-operate with managers of other departments but my co-operation seldom works out as well as I would like.

3. *Subordinates*
   When dealing with subordinates I attempt to combine both task and relationships consideration but one or the other often suffers.

4. *Staff advisers*
   I say I am willing to co-operate with staff advisers but do not always do so.

5. *Unions*
I say I want to co-operate with union representatives but sometimes put little effort into doing so.

6. *Customers*
I say that good relationships with customers should exist but I do not always do as much as I could to help matters.

7. *General public*
I say that good relationships with the general public are beneficial to the company but do little about maintaining them.

8. *Creativity*
I sometimes encourage new ideas but do not always follow up on too many of them.

9. *Objectives*
While my objectives are usually fairly clear, I allow them to be quite loose so they are not always a good guide.

10. *Planning*
I make an effort at planning but the plans do not always work out.

11. *Change introduction*
I sometimes talk about the problems of introducing change but do not always attempt to deal with these problems.

12. *Implementation*
I keep an eye on the implementation of plans but do not always take action when it is most needed.

13. *Controls*
I say that I believe control techniques are useful but I establish few and violate some.

14. *Evaluation*
I talk about the importance of evaluation and review but do not always get involved with it myself as much as I might.

15. *Productivity*
    I have some interest in higher productivity but it is not always apparent and thus productivity sometimes suffers.

16. *Communication*
    While I do try to keep an open channel of communication with others, I am not always successful in doing so.

17. *Conflict*
    When conflict arises I try to be fair but firm.

18. *Errors*
    I accept the fact that one can learn from errors but only occasionally do I put this to use.

19. *Meetings*
    I seem interested only in the task at some meetings and only in relationships at others.

20. *Teamwork*
    I like the idea of teamwork but often am not able to find ways to apply it.

11. Are you a bureaucrat?

To place and power all public spirit tends;
In place and power all public spirit ends.

Thomas Moore

He who is firmly seated in authority soon learns to think of security, and not progress, the highest lesson of statescraft.

Lowell

The bureaucrat manager (Exhibit 11.1) is one who is using a low task orientation and a low relationships orientation in a situation where such behaviour is appropriate and who is therefore more effective.

Exhibit 11.1 *The bureaucrat*

Bureaucrat indicators

- Follows orders, rules, procedures
- Reliable/dependable
- Maintains system and going concerns
- Watches details/efficient
- Rational/logical/self-controlled
- Fair/just/equitable
- Prefers to write out communications with others

- Responds to disagreement and conflict by referring to rules and procedures

Some things a bureaucrat might say include:

'The time is getting near for that report. Is it in good order and on schedule?'

'If we each know and carry out our own particular duties not much can go wrong.'

'I think we should try to exercise a little more creativity around here. Where is that memo on creativity from Head Office?'

'I like to stay within the bounds of past practice; this keeps everything on an even keel.'

'The really good thing about this company is that everything is laid down for you.'

'Look after the rules and regulations and the company will run itself.'

'Going through the right channels is the mark of the effective manager.'

'Follow the rules and you'll never go far wrong.'

'Let's see how we did it last time; that is usually the best way.'

'Clear rules and procedures are the basic elements of efficiency.'

'I believe that formal meetings are a perfectly sound way to produce new ideas.'

'Decide what is best and then make sure it is followed closely.'

Bureaucrat behaviour and effects

The bureaucrat style is simply the separated style used appropriately. Bureaucrat managers are essentially ones who use separated behaviour in a separated situation. Bureaucrats are not overly interested in either task or relationships. They are effective however in that their position or situation does not require this sort of interest; they get less personally involved with the problems of others.

The bureaucrat style was first written about by Max Weber, the Austrian sociologist. He proposed that the bureaucrat is an ideal style. He thought that it was the right way to do things and many organizations are modelled on it now.

'Bureaucrat' has unfortunately become a negative term in most management literature. Many people do not appear to recognize or accept the fact that the bureaucrat style is a key style in maintaining the effectiveness of modern organizations. Rules are needed to harness the efforts of more than a small face-to-face group. A device is also needed to see that all know the rules and follow them. Bureaucrats are often this device.

Bureaucratic managers are efficient. They go through the right channels, are sticklers for detail, and follow orders exactly. Their orientation is to the rules of the game. If they are managers, they see standard operating procedures in the same light. For them, existing and past practice are the guidelines to follow. True bureaucrats are highly successful organization members. They keep the going concern in order. The rules, none of which they may have established, they follow. It is no different from any sport.

While effective in following the rules, bureaucrat managers produce few ideas, do not push for production, and do a poor job of developing subordinates. Either their job does not require these qualities or it requires them to a minimal degree.

Bureaucrats and even deserters are sometimes incorrectly appraised as autocrats. All three of these styles have a low relationships orientation, but only the autocrat has a high task orientation. What some people mistake for task orientation is often adherence to outmoded rules at a heavy expense to the individuals involved. This behaviour is simply being nasty.

The bureaucratic style is effective in many situations. It might help to make it more acceptable if it were called the administrator style. Bureaucrat is the more established term however. It also tells it like it is.

Your bureaucrat score and how to change it

Your score

Turn back to Exhibit 3.1 to obtain your adjusted score on the bureaucrat scale. It is the last line under E. If your score is 11 or above, it indicates that you have a dominant style of bureaucrat. That is, it is a style you use frequently. If your score is 10 you have a supporting style of bureaucrat. That is, a style you resort to fairly frequently. If your score is four or below you are over-rejecting the bureaucrat style, that is, you use it very little if at all.

At this point only one style is being considered. After you have looked at each of your eight styles individually the styles will be looked at together as a style profile.

It is important to remind you, yet again, that this test measures your behaviour in the job you now have. If your score is high on this style it is not indicative that you are like it permanently. This is not a test of personality; it is a test of your behaviour in the job you now have.

Changing your behaviour

The statements below reflect bureaucrat behaviour. As you see, they reflect bureaucrat behaviour with all of the twenty situational elements described in Exhibit 5.3. Should you wish to increase your bureaucrat score then change your behaviour with respect to one or more of these.

1. *Superior*
   I believe that there will be few problems between myself and higher management if proper procedures and channels are followed.

2. *Coworkers*
   I prefer to go through the right channels when working with managers of associated departments.

3. *Subordinates*
   I think that things go best when subordinates understand and follow the duties in their job description.

4. *Staff advisers*
   I follow company policy and procedures when dealing with staff advisers.

5. *Unions*
   I believe the best way to maintain good union relationships is for both sides to follow the agreement exactly as it is written.

6. *Customers*
   I follow general company policy in maintaining customer relationships.

7. *General public*
   I believe in following past practice when dealing with the general public.

8. *Creativity*
   I believe that formal meetings are a perfectly sound way to produce new ideas.

9. *Objectives*
   Objectives I set are clear and inflexible.

10. *Planning*
    I plan with a fine attention to detail.

11. *Change introduction*
    I introduce changes formally and follow closely any established procedures.

12. *Implementation*
    Once plans are made I make sure that their implementation follows the original plan very closely.

13. *Controls*
    I believe that tight controls are a sound way to increase productivity.

14. *Evaluation*
    I emphasize regular evaluation, measurement and review of performance.

15. *Productivity*
    I believe that the best measure of output is a comparison based on standards previously established.

16. *Communication*
    I prefer to write out communications with others.

17. *Conflict*
    I respond to disagreement and conflict by referring to rules and procedures.

18. *Errors*
    I believe that errors would be minimal if people simply followed established rules and procedures.

19. *Meetings*
    I believe formal meetings are the best ones.

20. *Teamwork*
    I think that the team approach is of use at times but that formal meetings accomplish as much or even more.

12. Are you a developer?

> I will pay more for the ability to deal with people than any other ability under the sun.
>
> *John D. Rockefeller*

> The average human being learns, under proper conditions, not only to accept but to seek responsibility.
>
> *Douglas McGregor*

The developer manager (Exhibit 12.1) is one who is using a high relationships orientation and a low task orientation in a situation where such behaviour is appropriate and who is therefore more effective.

Exhibit 12.1 *The developer*

Developer indicators

- Maintains open communication channels
- Develops talent of others/coaches
- Understands others/supports
- Works well with others/co-operates
- Trusted by others/trusts/listens
- When responsible for planning, involves many others

Some things a developer might say include:

> 'About that report, do you need any assistance from me in order to do a good job?'

'My job is to tap the creativity and ingenuity of my subordinates.'

'The fewer direct controls on individuals the greater the likelihood of motivation and quality production.'

'If employees do not grow to accept new responsibility, it is often the fault of the boss.'

'Leaders are best when people barely know they exist.'

'People want to work: my job is to create the situation where they can.'

'My main interest is in finding better ways to coach my subordinates.'

'Managers should be judged by their subordinates' growth.'

Developer behaviour and effects

The developer style arises when the related style is being used appropriately. Developer managers are generally seen as those who place implicit trust in people. This is the effective version of the related style. The main difference between the missionary and the developer is that the latter is effective in motivating and working with people. Developers see their job as concerned primarily with developing the talents of others and of providing a work atmosphere conducive to their subordinates' commitment to both themselves and the job.

The developer is someone who uses relationships orientation in the service of subordinates and also of the situation. It is someone who is a helpful coach, sometimes seen as the invisible person in the organization. Developers are often quiet, unassuming and self-effacing. They may work with teams, they may work with individuals but the emphasis, sometimes quite unconsciously, is always as a developer of others.

General Electric Company invited outside interviewers to ask 300 of its managers what had been most important in their development. Ninety per cent answered in terms of working for a particular superior at some point in their career. This is heavy metal.

In most organizations, developer managers have very low visibility. They just sit there turning engineers into general managers, and no one recognizes it. Their job is seen by all as a very pleasant one because there is usually so much cooperation in their own and in associated departments. Their skill in creating such a condition often goes unnoticed.

Developers spend a lot of time with their subordinates. They give them as many new responsibilities as they can. They know that average people in industry are producing far below their capacity, but they also know how to motivate them to produce more.

Developers are seen as having some interesting assumptions about work. They believe that work is as natural as play or rest, that people want to exercise self-direction and self-control, and that they seek responsibility. They believe what is hard for many managers to believe: that intelligence, imagination and creativity are widely distributed in the population and are not possessed solely by senior managers.

Developer managers can motivate others to peak performance because subordinates see themselves doing it for them and with them. Developers tend to produce a creative atmosphere. They deliberately weaken the impact of the existing organization or job structure, and this allows their individual subordinates more freedom to think of new ideas. Their openness to novelty and their genuine interest in subordinate self-expression fosters creativity more.

One research study we did involved 1700 managers in more than 100 different companies. One thing we looked at was what style occurs disproportionately at the top and what style earns disproportionately more. The answer, to both questions, was the developer. The developer style is more often seen at the top of organizations and those who have the developer style were earning more. We looked at a very high salary bracket figure and a highly disproportionate amount of those were developers. Obviously, this is not, in any way, suggesting that other styles will not routinely get to the top and that other styles will not routinely earn more. But the facts are there. The developer won on level in hierarchy and won on salary level. True.

Your developer score and how to change it

Your score

Turn back to Exhibit 3.1 to obtain your adjusted score on the developer scale. It is the last line under F. If your score is 11 or above, it indicates that you have a dominant style of developer. That is, it is a style you use frequently. If your score is 10 you have a supporting style of developer. That is, a style you resort to fairly frequently. If your score is four or below you are over-rejecting the developer style, that is, you use it very little if at all.

At this point only one style is being considered. After you have looked at each of your eight styles individually the styles will be looked at together as a style profile.

It is important to remind you, yet again, that this test measures your behaviour in the job you now have. If your score is high on this style it is not indicative that you are like it permanently. This is not a test of personality; it is a test of your behaviour in the job you now have.

Changing your behaviour

The statements below reflect developer behaviour. As you see, they reflect developer behaviour with all of the 20 situational elements described in Exhibit 5.3. Should you wish to increase your developer score then change your behaviour with respect to one or more of these.

1. *Superior*
   I understand and co-operate well with higher level management.

2. *Coworkers*
   I work to maintain good relationships with other departments.

3. *Subordinates*
   My relationship with subordinates is excellent and is characterized by mutual trust and respect.

4. *Staff advisers*
   I understand and co-operate well with staff advisers.

5. *Unions*
   I am effective in encouraging trusting union–management relationships.

6. *Customers*
   I believe that the opinions of customers are of prime concern to the company.

7. *General public*
   I believe in encouraging all concerned to present the company to the public in a good light.

8. *Creativity*
I seek out new and good ideas and motivate others to be as creative as possible.

9. *Objectives*
I successfully motivate others to set their own clear objectives.

10. *Planning*
When I am responsible for planning I involve many others.

11. *Change introduction*
I prepare those affected by change by talking to them well in advance.

12. *Implementation*
I am responsive to sound proposals for modifying plans, am open to suggestions and am always willing to help.

13. *Controls*
I believe that performance data is best fed back to the individual concerned rather than to the superior.

14. *Evaluation*
I encourage others to evaluate their own and my own performance.

15. *Productivity*
I motivate others to set high output standards and encourage and support them so that these high standards are met.

16. *Communication*
I maintain open, trusting communication channels with everyone.

17. *Conflict*
When conflict arises I help those involved to find a sound basis for agreement.

18. *Errors*
I think that most errors arise for a good reason and it is better to look for the reason than at the error itself.

19. *Meetings*
    I make many suggestions at meetings and encourage others to do the same.

20. *Teamwork*
    I believe in the team approach to the extent that I think most problems are best solved that way.

13. Are you a benevolent autocrat?

I once heard a manager say, 'I am going to make this department participative no matter how hard I have to push to do it.'

A very useful sales incentive plan at times is, 'If you get to meet your quota, you get to keep your job.'

The benevolent autocrat manager (Exhibit 13.1) is one who is using a high task orientation and a low relationships orientation in a situation where such behaviour is appropriate and who is therefore more effective.

Exhibit 13.1 *The benevolent autocrat*

Benevolent autocrat indicators

- Decisive/shows initiative
- Industrious/energetic
- Finisher/committed
- Evaluative of quantity, quality and time
- Costs, profits and sales conscious
- Obtains results
- Both develops and proposes many new ideas
- Shows that efficiency and productivity are valued

Some things a benevolent autocrat might say include:

'The boss is asking about that report. Let me have a memo

immediately on its current status, your problems, if any, and your anticipated completion date.'

'I like to walk fairly softly but still carry a big stick.'

'I prefer to make up my own mind but will sometimes ask my subordinates for ideas.'

'The best managers are those who work their way up and learn about the best ways of achieving production from the mistakes they made in being tough at times.'

'A good manager keeps a clear eye on the output of all the subordinates.'

'Promotion and pay raises should be based exclusively on output.'

'A tough minded disagreement with a fellow manager over how best a task is to be done is a sure sign of productive decision making even though feelings might get hurt.'

Benevolent autocrat behaviour and effects

The benevolent autocrat is task-oriented, intervenes a great deal and is effective. It is not a style to use in the administration section of an insurance company or managing independent professionals, such as in a tax office or an R & D laboratory or a university. It is more likely to be useful in a steel mill. As an example of the benevolent autocrat, General Patton once said, 'Everyone needs a pat on the back from time to time—but some need it lower than others.'

Benevolent autocrat managers are usually perceived as ones who place implicit trust in themselves and in their own way of doing things. They are concerned about, and effective in, obtaining high production in both the short and long run. Their main skill is getting other people to do what they want them to do without creating undue resentment. They are seen as having much of the orientation of the autocrat in terms of personal style, but it is clear to all that it is not to serve their own needs that they push others around; they are serving the organization's needs for higher productivity.

This style is a popular one in industry today. It often characterizes managers who have worked up through the company ranks and who have attempted to improve their skill by learning from their errors. Benevolent autocrats are usually somewhat ambitious, know the company methods very well, stay on top of their jobs, and get the jobs done.

Benevolent autocrats in top management have little sympathy

with participation or bottom–up management. They will sometimes use a participative approach before reaching their decision but not after it. They know that allowing subordinates to comment beforehand may produce a good idea, will alert them to problems they must deal with, and almost always will reduce resistance to change.

The benevolent autocrat style is likely to be effective when managers have responsibility; when they have power and a reward-and-punishment system; when they have to give orders for the system to work; and when they have more knowledge than their subordinates. The style is facilitated further if the subordinates expect to be managed in a dedicated fashion and if they lack knowledge or decision making capability.

Some people through charm, a long run view, obvious competence, or personal example can make the dedicated style effective in many quite different situations. What happens, in fact, is that subordinates accept the style as appropriate for their managers. They may still call them 'hardnosed' and 'drivers' but nevertheless will be committed to them and their plans.

Your benevolent autocrat style and how to change it

Your score
Turn back to Exhibit 3.1 to obtain your adjusted score on the benevolent autocrat scale. It is the last line under G. If your score is 11 or above, it indicates that you have a dominant style of benevolent autocrat. That is, it is a style you use frequently. If your score is 10 you have a supporting style of benevolent autocrat. That is, a style you resort to fairly frequently. If your score is four or below you are over-rejecting the benevolent autocrat style, that is, you use it very little if at all.

At this point only one style is being considered. After you have looked at each of your eight styles individually the styles will be looked at together as a style profile.

It is important to remind you, yet again, that this test measures your behaviour in the job you now have. If your score is high on this style it is not indicative that you are like it permanently. This is not a test of personality, it is a test of your behaviour in the job you now have.

Changing your behaviour
The statements below reflect benevolent autocrat behaviour. As you

see, they reflect benevolent autocrat behaviour with all of the situational elements described in Exhibit 5.3. Should you wish to increase your benevolent autocrat score then change your behaviour with respect to one or more of these.

1. *Superior*
   I work well with higher level management and ensure that they know exactly how I see my job.

2. *Coworkers*
   I am open to suggestions from other departments and use what I personally believe to be the best ideas.

3. *Subordinates*
   I make clear to subordinates what I expect of them. I show that I value efficiency and productivity.

4. *Staff advisers*
   I believe staff advisers must prove that their suggestions will increase productivity.

5. *Unions*
   I respect unions and they respect me. My thoughts on union–management relationships are put over effectively.

6. *Customers*
   I believe that the company should first produce a good product and then get the customer to accept it.

7. *General public*
   I believe that all employees should present the company to the public as being a good corporate citizen.

8. *Creativity*
   I both develop and propose many new ideas.

9. *Objectives*
   I personally set clear objectives that are understood by all those involved.

10. *Planning*
    I plan well and concentrate primarily on my own good ideas and assign individual responsibilities.

11. *Change introduction*
I inform all concerned of the reasons for a change.

12. *Implementation*
I watch the implementation of plans by individuals and give direct assistance and guidance where needed.

13. *Controls*
I show that I think good control techniques are among the most important keys to a high productivity.

14. *Evaluation*
I keep methods and output under constant review and make changes to ensure high output.

15. *Productivity*
I personally set high output standards for myself and others and work hard to see that they are met.

16. *Communication*
I keep everyone fully informed of what I think they need to know in order to do their jobs better.

17. *Conflict*
When facing conflict I stand my ground and try to be as persuasive as possible.

18. *Errors*
I think the best way to minimize errors is for those making them to have their errors explained.

19. *Meetings*
I take an active and useful part in meetings and use them to push successfully for my ideas.

20. *Teamwork*
I believe in the team approach but also believe a good team needs a good leader who knows what is to be done.

14. Are you an executive?

The executive manager (Exhibit 14.1) is one who is using a high task orientation and a high relationships orientation in a situation where such behaviour is appropriate and who is therefore more effective.

Exhibit 14.1 *The executive manager*

Executive indicators

- Uses teamwork in decision making
- Uses participation appropriately
- Induces commitment to objectives
- Encourages higher performance
- Co-ordinates others in work

Some things an executive might say include:

'I aim for true involvement and by it obtain commitment to optimum output.'

'In some situations I announce my decision after hearing ideas; in other situations the team works for concensus.'

'High output standards, clear quality controls and high subordinate motivation and commitment are the marks of a good manager.'

'I want my subordinates to produce at their optimum, which I realize may vary widely from one to another.'

'My job is to obtain the best thinking of all and to get everyone to translate this into optimum production.'

'Optimum production involves both an understanding and utilization of the human and the task variables.'

'A good manager can always make the standards known without impairing the subordinates' approach to their jobs.'

'True team management, in the long run, is the most effective.'

'To obtain optimum production managers sometimes have to treat everyone somewhat differently.'

Executive behaviour and effects

Executive managers are seen by their subordinates as being personally interested in them and as wanting to improve their effectiveness. The subordinates have confidence in their superiors and see them as attempting to build an effective organization.

The executive style is usually reflected in the behaviour of the managers who see their jobs as maximizing effectively the efforts of others in relation to both short and long run tasks. They set high standards for production and performance but recognize that because of individual differences they will have to treat everyone differently. They are effective in that their commitment to both task and relationships is evident to all and acts as a powerful motivating force.

Executive managers welcome disagreement and conflict over task problems. They see such behaviour as necessary, normal, and appropriate. They do not suppress, deny, or avoid conflict. They believe that differences can be worked through, that conflict can be solved, and that commitment will result when both are done. Executive managers know their own jobs and want others to know their own jobs.

Executive management is often team management. Executive managers believe in the interdependence of job functions and work to produce a smoothly functioning, efficiently working team. They initiate many things by group action. Often they are seen as creative and as innovators, but, in fact, it is their teams that produce the ideas owing to the climate the executive managers have induced.

They arouse participation and by it obtain commitment. They

strive to obtain involvement in planning and to obtain the best thinking possible. They know that any mature person has a need for both dependence and independence and that individual needs and organization goals can be meshed.

Although executives are good managers, they have an, essentially, colleague or coworker orientation. They work particularly well when there are only low power differences between themselves and others—when only expertise has influence. They want to respond to the actual demands of the sociotechnical system in which they find themselves. They do not want to be bothered with what they see as artificial elements such as status differences.

Executive managers prefer equality in management to differences of status and power. They lead by inducing their subordinates to commit themselves to common objectives rather than to the manager or to their own duties.

Executive managers build loyalty among their subordinates. In doing so, they develop in all of them a keen sense of self-respect which they are reluctant to lose. This, itself, adds another strong tie to the service of organization objectives.

The executive style is the one that is proclaimed most as the ideal style. It is Blake's 9.9, McGregor's Theory Y and Likert's System 4. It is not the only style to use. There are many different jobs in organizations. There are jobs where other styles may be more appropriate.

Clearly, the executive style is needed in managing interacting managers. Its use is virtually demanded when managers must decide on the optimum distribution of scarce resources among them.

Your executive score and how to change it

Your score

Turn back to Exhibit 3.1 to obtain your adjusted score on the executive scale. It is the last line under H. If your score is 11 or above, it indicates that you have a dominant style of executive. That is, it is a style you use frequently. If your score is 10 you have a supporting style of executive. That is, a style you resort to fairly frequently. If your score is four or below you are over-rejecting the executive style, that is, you use it very little if at all.

At this point only one style is being considered. After you have looked at each of your eight styles individually the styles will be looked at together as a style profile.

It is important to remind you, yet again, that this test measures your behaviour in the job you now have. If your score is high on this style it is not indicative that you are like it permanently. This is not a test of personality, it is a test of your behaviour in the job you now have.

Changing your behaviour
The statements below reflect executive behaviour. As you see, they reflect executive behaviour with all of the 20 situational elements described in Exhibit 5.3. Should you wish to increase your executive score then change your behaviour with respect to one or more of these.

1. *Superior*
   I believe higher management is best seen as part of other teams that should interlock effectively with my own.

2. *Coworkers*
   All interdepartmental differences in which I am involved are solved jointly.

3. *Subordinates*
   I demonstrate that I expect high output from my subordinates yet recognize and consider individual differences.

4. *Staff advisers*
   I see staff advisers as sources of competent help and welcome suggestions from them.

5. *Unions*
   My actual relationships with union representatives demonstrate that I have a commitment to both productivity and productive union–management relationships.

6. *Customers*
   I believe a fundamental goal of the firm is to create customers.

7. *General public*
   I work with all concerned to present the company in the best possible light to the general public.

8. *Creativity*
   I am constantly on the watch for new, useful and productive ideas from any source and develop many new ideas myself.

9. *Objectives*
   I set objectives with others which are clear and fully agreed to by all those directly involved.

10. *Planning*
    When I am involved the plans made represent the best thinking of all concerned.

11. *Change introduction*
    I inform all concerned well in advance of any possible changes and give them an opportunity to influence the proposed change.

12. *Implementation*
    I keep an eye on the implementation of plans and respond quickly to, and solve, any blockages.

13. *Controls*
    If a procedure or control is violated I make sure I concentrate on finding out why.

14. *Evaluation*
    I have both methods and output under constant review and changes in them are regularly implemented as needed.

15. *Productivity*
    I set high standards for myself and encourage others to set high output standards.

16. *Communication*
    I have an open communication channel with everyone on any matter and others have it with me.

17. *Conflict*
    I try to resolve conflict as quickly as possible by uncovering its underlying causes.

18. *Errors*

I treat errors primarily as opportunities for everyone to learn and am prepared to look openly at my own errors.

19. *Meetings*

I use meetings to arrive at the best possible decisions to which everyone is committed.

20. *Teamwork*

I actively support and promote the team approach to management.

15. What is your style profile?

This chapter will give you an opportunity to look at your eight styles together. It contains a chart for you to display them together and gives actual examples of the profiles of others to help you with the interpretation.

You should transfer your adjusted scores from the bottom line in Exhibit 3.1 to the chart in Exhibit 15.1. Simply shade in a vertical line to indicate your adjusted score on each of the eight styles.

Dominant, supporting and over-reject styles

Notice that there are three words to the left of the chart. These are dominant, supporting and over-reject. The dominant and supporting styles have been discussed before. The over-reject style is one which you tend to lean away from, more than most managers. This also is worth looking at. It is what you really do not like doing.

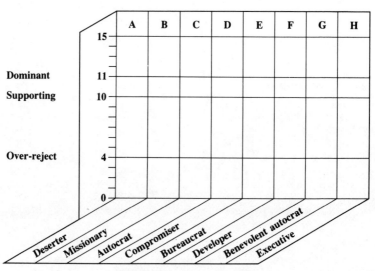

Exhibit 15.1 *Your style profile*

Your dominant style

Your dominant style is a managerial style which you use a great deal. It is represented by a score of 11 or more. For some managers the dominant style is very easy to detect by simply observing their work behaviour. They are clearly bureaucrats or autocrats or whatever. Some managers have no dominant style, some have three and sometimes even more. This may be because of the variety of demands in their jobs. For instance, it may be that they have a role in supervising some kind of administrative type work and also some production type work. This normally requires two different styles and might well explain two quite different dominant styles. Some jobs require supervision of both sales people and customers. Some work requires supervision of scientists and also clerical workers. So, multiple dominant styles can arise from these different job components. They can equally arise also from the way a manager operates in a single job component. Two dominant styles, say missionary and deserter, would indicate a 'friendly bystander'. Two dominant styles of bureaucrat and autocrat indicate that the manager expects to be able to say, 'Do it my way—or else.' So, in looking at your dominant styles think about the various pairs of them as well as looking at them individually.

Some managers have either no dominant more effective style or no dominant less effective style, or neither. If there is no dominant more effective style it may well indicate style flexibility. That is, a variety of styles are being used appropriately. If there is no dominance in the less effective styles it may indicate style drift. That is, a variety of styles are being used inappropriately.

Your supporting style

Your supporting style is any style with a score of ten. In short, it indicates a style that is used more than average. It is a style you make above average use of compared to other managers. It is not so important to interpret as is the dominant style or over-rejected style.

Your over-rejected styles

An over-rejected style is any style which a manager uses far less frequently than the average manager. It is represented by a score of four or less. Obviously, over-rejection is desirable when the over-rejected style is less effective. Some managers, however, reject such styles as developer or benevolent autocrat. This may indicate, but not necessarily, that there is an unwillingness or incapacity to use these styles when in fact the situation might require it. Look at your over-rejected styles as closely as you do your dominant styles. If you have a dominant style of benevolent autocrat and you over-reject missionary this combination does give a far clearer indication of just how tough-minded you are. Here are some brief notes on over-rejection of each of the eight managerial styles.

Deserter   An over-rejection of the deserter style indicates an unwillingness to avoid the situation. You do not use situation avoidance as a means of being less effective. It might help to see in what ways you are in fact less effective if you are not using this particular style.

Missionary   An over-rejection of the missionary style indicates your unwillingness to become dependent on the situation. It might be that some of your dominant styles, whether less effective or more effective, might lead to this in some way. As previously indicated, if you over-reject missionary and are dominant on benevolent autocrat, these things can be put together and interpreted to strengthen the point about your single-minded toughness. However, if you over-reject missionary and are dominant on developer this would tend to indicate that your developer style arises not from a simple love of people and wanting to be loved by them, but from a tough-minded approach to developing others in the work situation.

Autocrat   An over-rejection of the autocrat style indicates your unwillingness to put productivity before people in a crude, mindless way. You do not attack situations you do not like, you deal with them in other ways. Again, compare this with your dominant styles as well.

Compromiser   Your over-rejection of the compromiser style indicates that you successfully avoid those situations where you may try and not succeed. An over-rejection of compromiser might also indicate a low tolerance of ambiguity and a strong desire to be successful.

Bureaucrat   Your over-rejection of the bureaucratic style indicates the lack of use of methods orientation as a means of becoming more effective. The possible reasons are that your position may not demand such orientation, or that perhaps it does and you do not realize it, or that you simply do not like methods and rules. Low score on bureaucrat can indicate a maverick in an organization, someone who is counter-dependent and simply does not want to play by the rules. The supposition is that you can get away with it. In some it creates difficulties. In some organizations mavericks do not advance or even last, while in some they are welcome. A low score on bureaucratic orientation is sometimes related to having problems in being effective with one's superior. That is rather obvious, is it not?

Developer   The over-rejection of the developer style indicates a lack of use of people orientation as a means of becoming more effective. It might be that your position does not demand it, or that it does and you do not realize it, or that you do not obtain satisfaction from being people-oriented. Another explanation may be lack of skill in being people-oriented. Some light can be thrown on this if you, again, compare it with your dominant style.

Benevolent autocrat   The over-rejection of the benevolent autocrat style indicates a lack of use of results orientation as a means of becoming more effective. Lack of use of this style may be explained in much the same way as indicated for the bureaucrat style and developer style.

Executive   The over-rejection of the executive style indicates a lack of use of team orientation as a means of becoming more effective. Again, think of the reasons why this might occur and compare it with your dominant style.

Illustrative style profiles

This section provides some illustrative style profiles of other actual managers. You may find these helpful in thinking about your own style profile.

Missionary–Developer
The manager whose style profile is shown in Exhibit 15.2 has a dominant double style of missionary–developer and over-rejects styles of deserter and benevolent autocrat. The job was as a training manager.

This profile fits very well for that kind of role. The job is working with people and attempting to develop them. The role does not

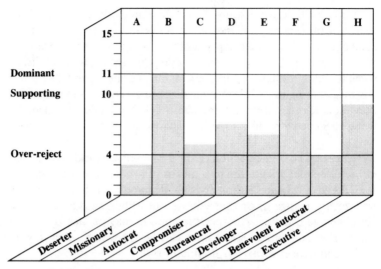

Exhibit 15.2   *A missionary–developer. A training manager profile*

necessarily require a high score on missionary but of any of the three less effective styles this would probably be the better one. The over-rejection of benevolent autocrat also fits the work role very well: there is not really very much a training manager or development officer can be benevolent autocrat about. It is quite typical for those in training functions to have high scores in missionary, developer and executive. This manager uses the related style when less effective and the related style when more effective.

Missionary–Autocrat
The manager in the process of installing an incompany computer system developed the profile shown in Exhibit 15.3.

This profile almost certainly arose from what this particular manager saw as the best way to install a computer system. The manager had decided that the best way was to thrust the computer down the throats of all, and by pushing so hard produced a strong negative reaction. Things got so bad that little could be done without signed orders from the CEO. The style used impaired the manager's health and the stress undergone caused a heart attack. The way of dealing with the resistance met, which was self-created, was to use yet another less effective style of missionary. The basic problem was that of low situational sensitivity. How else could you

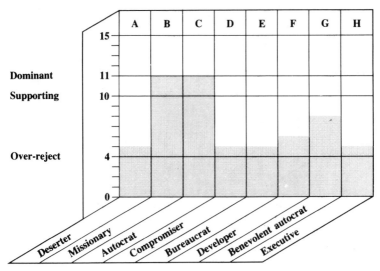

Exhibit 15.3 *A missionary–autocrat. Low situational sensitivity can be inferred from this profile*

explain someone who is less effective in two completely different styles? Remaining with the firm, this manager changed style to that of a more natural benevolent autocrat. This profile represents the way this manager tackled a particular job: the wrong way.

Deserter–Executive

Double dominant of deserter–executive seems strange but it does occur (Exhibit 15.4). This manager was a somewhat selfish, self-centred university administrator who also had a teaching post.

This administrator was loved by students and was, without question, an excellent teacher and was also much liked by junior colleagues but more senior colleagues were not so sure. The administrator was highly self-confident but somewhat frail in the face of adversity, and as the centre of attention in a somewhat dominant position acted extremely well as a team leader. This explains the good relationships with students and junior colleagues. However when under threat or stress this administrator moved to desertion, but being quite creative about how this was done, only a reasonably close observer would notice. When applying for the second most senior administrative post in the university this manager found enormous general support, but did not get the much

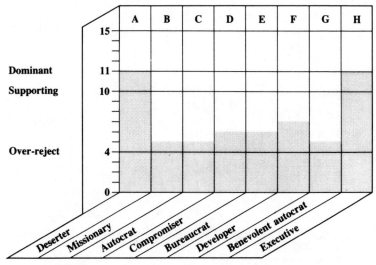

Exhibit 15.4   *A deserter–executive. A good manager sometimes*

needed support from senior colleagues who controlled the committee. Having failed to get the job this administrator at first went on leave from the university and, finally, did not return. This is a clear case of dominant double deserter and executive. If you cannot win, you sulk. If you get your own way you are a winner. If you do not get your own way you are a loser.

An extreme profile

Profiles as extreme as in Exhibit 15.5 occur occasionally. In this case those styles with relationships orientation in them were extremely high and all those without were extremely low. This extremeness obviously suggests both resilience and rigidity: resilience where the job had high relationships demands and rigidity where it did not. This manager tried once to go into sales and failed. While some people think that sales staff need high relationships orientation, this is really artificial. It is often a façade. This manager was so extreme, being unable to use a relationships façade, it had to be relationships, and the particular selling job did not require this. This manager was most successful at working for the national government in setting up special training courses running up to a year, for unemployed youths and adults, and, although not doing much of the actual training, managed to do an excellent job in gathering community resources.

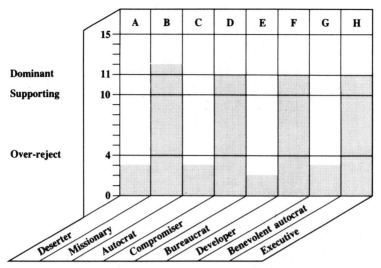

Exhibit 15.5 *An extreme profile*

Flat profile

A flat profile as shown in Exhibit 15.6 is best interpreted as the use of a wide variety of behaviours. It might arise by job demands, style flexibility, or style drift. The frequent cause of the flat distribution is simply that the manager is highly responsive to a situation; both the actual task demands in it and also the people in it. Some managers are concerned when they see a flat distribution and ask something like, 'Am I really a manager with a distribution like this?' The answer is yes, you are. Only a closer study of the job itself and the way you perceive how it should be approached can lead to an adequate interpretation of this style profile. Other reasons for this style profile arising include that the job, in fact, has very low style demands and you can achieve effectiveness in a wide variety of ways. Again, study of the job is necessary.

Using the test organization-wide

Tests like this one obviously have a wide variety of uses. This one is being used here to help you to gain insight into your managerial style so you can think about how you may become more effective. There are other uses, however, as follows:

To create awareness of, and interest in, management styles

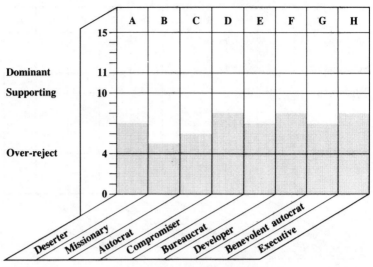

Exhibit 15.6   *A flat profile indicating flexibility and drift. Perhaps it is situation or perhaps it is drift*

To unfreeze managers, prior to individual or team training programmes

To personalize and thus stimulate discussion on management style

To establish a readiness to experience a personal development programme

To determine development and training needs

To provide the manager with a reasonably objective report of the styles used

To provide a starting point for coaching between associates or superior–subordinate pairs

To appraise important stylistic differences between work teams, departments, or companies

To appraise the nature of individual or company style modification over time

To corroborate or invalidate information about one's style that has been received from other sources

To determine the stylistic features of an organization's hierarchy, preparatory to an organization change programme

Most readers of this book are reading it for personal development. Some are thinking organization wide. Some may want to use the test to get a clear picture of styles in the organization as a whole.

This can help direct plan change efforts. If the company turns out to be 20 per cent bureaucratic and it thought it should be something else, then the test results can help only if they are followed by an action plan.

Things to do with these test results

You may have read this book privately or you may have read it as part of a public or incompany training course. In either case, here are some ideas to help you think more about your test results. It certainly helps if you discuss the results with other people. This may be your seminar syndicate team, or your superior, subordinates or coworkers. Be careful when you talk about it with your family. While we recommend this, older children (in particular) and spouses will often say something like, 'I could have told you that years ago!' It will also help if you make some kind of formal plan of which styles you would like to change and how you might like to change them.

Why not also write down why you think certain styles have arisen and whether you think you have the capacity to be flexible to change them and whether you should? Obviously, encourage others you work with, namely superiors, subordinates and coworkers, to complete the test themselves and to discuss it together.

A separately printed version of this test is available. It includes full scoring instructions and extensive interpretations. It is designed to be used in management training courses. For local supplier, write to: Organizational Tests Limited, P.O. Box 324, Fredericton, N.B. E3B 4Y9, Canada.

When the test results may be less accurate

Some circumstances can make the test results less accurate. If you are not a manager or supervisor, then, to a degree, you were imagining a position. If you are new in the job, then you may be finding your feet and, sometimes, the less effective styles are higher, compromiser in particular. The final and most important reason is the accuracy with which you see your own style. Chapter 3 contains the management style diagnosis test. This is a good test and widely used. However, because of its relative brevity and construction, some style scores may not always be correct. Also available from the address above is information on a test correcting for this. It is called the Managerial Effectiveness Test.

PART 4

Your three managerial skills

Logically, three things follow from what you have read so far. The three skills of an effective manager are the ability to read a situation for what it really contains—situational sensitivity; to adapt to the situation if needed—style flexibility; to change the situation if that is needed—situational management. This is not so new. A prayer attributed to St Francis of Assisi is:

> O Lord, give me the courage to change what should be changed, [situational management]
> The serenity to accept what cannot be changed, [style flexibility]
> And the wisdom to tell the difference, [situational sensitivity]

Effective managers understand that the key skill is in knowing what to do at a certain time in a certain situation. They know when to stand back, when to get involved, when to consult and when to make decisions. Perhaps the most difficult thing to grasp is simply when to say yes and when to say no. Sometimes they have to analyse. Sometimes they have to move with a situation. Sometimes they have to change it. Books cannot tell you what to do. All books can do is raise the issues with you. This part deals with the three managerial skills.

Situational sensitivity is the ability to read situations correctly, to appraise situational elements in terms of task and relationship demands, flexibility and strength.

The second skill, style flexibility, is the ability to employ a wide range of behaviour appropriately so that managerial effectiveness increases.

Situational management is the ability to change the demands of situational elements so that managerial effectiveness increases. The smooth introduction of change, through overcoming resistance in oneself and others, is a central management skill.

16. You and your situational sensitivity

To be great, to be a person of stature, a man must have character, judgment, high intelligence, a special aptitude for seeing his problems whole and true—for seeing things as they are, without exaggeration or emotion.

Field Marshal Montgomery

How can we avoid the two extremes; too great bossism in giving orders, and practically no orders given? . . . My solution is to depersonalize the giving of orders, to unite all concerned in a study of the situation, to discover the law of the situation and obey that.

Mary Parker Follett

Your situational sensitivity is your skill in reading a situation for what it really contains. Obviously, a key managerial skill is the ability to size up a situation. A manager with the sensitivity to read a situation for what it actually contains, and the sensitivity to know what behaviour would actually constitute effectiveness in it, is more likely to be effective.

Age and experience do tend to improve situation sensitivity as this skill is a component of experience. However, young managers sometimes show a brilliant understanding of situations and of what must be done to produce effectiveness. They know when to push hard, when not to, whom to see and the appropriate timing. Sensitive managers will know what resistances stand in the way of being effective and what they can overcome and must overcome to be effective. Although situational sensitivity is seldom perfect, managers can learn ways to improve it.

Sensitivity requires alertness and curiosity. Sensitive managers fit scraps of information and hunches together. Like any scientist, they look at details to construct the whole. From a firebed and an arrowhead, an archaeologist reconstructs a civilization. From the way in which a policy is received by different divisions sensitive managers can construct the reality of power politics in an organization.

If a manager makes a series of interventions in situations which later prove effective, then it is highly probable the manager has a high sensitivity to situations. If not, the manager would have made the wrong moves. If, however, a manager does nothing, this alone does not indicate whether or not there is high or low sensitivity. One may know what is wrong but not know how to do anything about it.

Situational sensitivity is a diagnostic skill not an action skill. This simply means that a manager may score high on situational sensitivity and yet do nothing with the skill. The well-trained psychologist, sociologist, or anthropologist may have the highest possible situational sensitivity yet the lowest possible effectiveness as a manager. To be effective, the sensitivity must be matched with style flexibility or situational management, but preferably both.

Management training exercises are available which measure situational sensitivity with great precision. They consist of depicting a situation by a film or written case study and then asking the manager to make a series of observations concerning it.

Do not trust to luck

Many highly sensitive managers, politicians or, for that matter, entrepreneurs are often described as lucky. The term 'luck', like magic, is really a device simply to explain what is to some an otherwise inexplicable outcome. Luck seldom explains managerial effectiveness. The manager in the right place at the right time with the appropriate resources did not come there solely by chance, although it may appear that way. They very often understood the existing or potential situation and were prepared for the opportunities as they came.

Managers with low sensitivity tend to have more difficulty than others in learning theories such as the 3-D theory of managerial effectiveness. The 3-D theory was designed to be reasonably free of bias and of any particular ideology save managerial effectiveness. Unlike many theories it does not suggest that flexibility, resilience or relationships are always good. It operates this way, in part, through the use of tight definitions and a situational approach. Some managers have difficulty in learning 3-D because they cannot see the difference between one situation and another. Without some skill at this level, it is impossible to understand the usefulness of 3-D, let alone have the skill to use it.

The causes of low situational sensitivity

While it may seem surprising to you, the main reason why you, or any manager, may have lower situational sensitivity than might be desirable is lack of knowledge about self. That is, low style awareness. If you distort yourself to yourself, that is, do not know where you stand or where you really are, you will automatically distort the situation as well. The first step, then, to improving situational sensitivity is to improve style awareness. Style awareness is the degree to which you appraise your own style correctly. It is knowledge of your impact on others, not of your impact on yourself. The prime usefulness of this self-knowledge is to enable you to make a more effective impact on the situation, not to allow you to marvel at your own psychic interior. Effective managers must know the impact they are having on others. Without this knowledge, they cannot assess the situation they are in and cannot predict the results of their own behaviour. Many types of group-dynamic management training courses attempt to, and usually can, improve style awareness, as can marriage or even children.

The fatal flaw

All of us have flaws; a few of us have fatal flaws which we seem condemned to keep repeating in different contexts. The flaw is best identified by looking at the situations which most often lead to more trouble than they should. The situation may involve a superior when the manager is in a low power situation, it may involve a coworker or a subordinate. It may involve planning, organizing, or controlling. It may be confronting disagreement, making a difficult decision, usually its postponement, trying to satisfy everyone, overreacting to criticism, being vague about poor performance or any one of many more. Fatal flaws often come disguised. The same basic flaw may have occurred in a dozen different ways. Only if a flaw is recognized can it be managed. It can be managed only by the person whose flaw it is.

Situational sensitivity alone

Situational sensitivity alone is of little value to the practising manager. If a manager cannot use the knowledge, then they may as well not have it. Those who go through life as hostile or as friendly observers of the scene are serving some need to appear intellectual rather than to be useful and, therefore, to be effective. One does not like to feel one is being analysed, and this is what situational sensitivity alone can lead to. Sensitivity must be related to an action programme of either managerial flexibility or situational management. Some managers have high sensitivity but low flexibility. They usually tend to change situations rather than change themselves. They use situational management.

Four parts of self

Everything known and not known about ourselves can be put under one of four headings:

1. What we know and others know—style awareness. (This is everyone's business.)
2. What others know and we do not know—style unawareness. (We must make this our business.)
3. What we know and others do not know—personal history. (This is our business only.)
4. What we and others do not know—unconscious. (This is no one's business.)

These can be arranged as demonstrated in Exhibit 16.1. The idea on which this exhibit is based (only the terminology is changed) was developed by two psychologists, Joe Luft and Harry Ingham. They call it the Johari Window.

This exhibit sharpens the importance of decreasing our degree of style unawareness. The style unawareness area is that part of our behaviour which others are well aware of but we are not. In simple terms, we may be acting in ways toward others, perhaps rejecting them, of which we are essentially unaware. Clearly, to be effective with others, we must know just what kind of impact we are making. To become more effective, then, a manager needs to make window 2 smaller by increasing the size of window 1.

Without a reasonable degree of style awareness, it is difficult to use management style concepts. Without knowing our own basic style, it is all too easy to distort the style of another or the basic-style demands of a situation itself.

Some questions for managers to ask themselves
Style awareness is difficult to improve by simply thinking about it, but some assistance may be obtained by answering each of the following questions honestly:

		Self of ourselves	
		Known	Not known
Others of ourselves	Known	**1** Style awareness	**2** Style unawareness
	Not known	**3** Personal history	**4** Unconscious

Exhibit 16.1 *Four parts of self. Everything about ourselves can be put in one of these four boxes. To improve their effectiveness, managers need to make box 1 bigger and box 2 smaller*

1. If someone said of you 'You sometimes act like a kid', what behaviour would they be thinking of?
2. What do you do that gets you into trouble?
3. Are there any major themes in your life which seem to repeat themselves, perhaps in different contexts?
4. Do you care more about yourself than others?
5. If you obtained a liveable pension today, would you still like to keep your job?
6. What did you do when your father was angry at you? Mother angry at you? Friends angry at you?
7. What does your spouse think of you? What do your children think of you?
8. What do you do when your superior is angry with you? Coworkers angry with you?
9. What do you typically do when under attack or faced with conflict?
10. What are your major disappointments in life?
11. What are your major disappointments at work?
12. Who is responsible for your major disappointments?
13. What made you proudest as a child? As an adult?

14. What is your favourite daydream? Do you see anything in it that might be making you a more or less effective manager?
15. What is your single major accomplishment?

Most of these questions tap the manager's underlying personality dynamics. They are questions we seldom think about. The answers to them differentiate us sharply from others.

Your defence mechanisms

For a variety of reasons we sometimes are unconsciously not interested in making a sound situational diagnosis. It may be that if we make a realistic diagnosis we will discover things we do not like, or things we simply do not want to know, or things we do not know how to handle. The main, unconscious mental protective devices we use are known as defence mechanisms, and were first identified as such by Sigmund Freud.

Defence mechanisms are not necessarily psychologically unhealthy. All healthy personalities need temporary protection from time to time. The problem occurs when the temporary protection turns into a permanent drop in situational sensitivity and so to a distortion of reality. The defence mechanisms operate entirely outside the awareness of some managers, operating in the unconscious, serving to hide or to shield them from what is unacceptable, threatening or repugnant in the situation so that these things become unrecognized or unacknowledged. In layman's language, defence mechanisms give us blind spots we unconsciously think we need.

The main defence mechanisms managers should be aware of in themselves and others are rationalization (inventing reasons) and projection ('It's you, not me').

In addition to the two mechanisms of rationalization and projection, the following five factors also lead to low sensitivity: negative adaptation (accepting things as they are), symptoms for causes (mistaking appearance for cause), lack of conceptual language (not talking the same language), limiting value system (having one test for everything), and high levels of anxiety (being a worrier).

Rationalization (inventing reasons)

Rationalization involves inventing plausible but spurious explanations. An example is attributing the promotion of someone to office politics when in fact the promotion was based on managerial effectiveness.

Rationalization involves inventing and accepting interpretations which an impartial analysis would not substantiate. It is kidding ourselves about what the world is really like. Rationalization serves to conceal our view of the situation in such a way that the problem is seen as in the situation, not in ourselves. The justification of such interpretation usually involves giving socially acceptable reasons for behaviour or apparently logical reasons for the view of the situation. In business life, what is rationalized in this way is usually believed by the manager but is often not understood or believed by the listener.

All managers are familiar with rationalization. They see it in the manager passed over for promotion who decided it was not wanted anyway. This is called 'sour grapes', after the fable about the fox who could not get at some grapes and who then decided they were sour. Managers who continually 'sour grape' turn into one.

Rationalization is not rare. Some managers use it so much that it incapacitates them; most use it to some extent: 'The job was not completed because other things came up', 'The promotion was missed because the superior was biased', 'The subordinates were fired because they were incompetent.'

The problem with rationalization is not so much that we fool ourselves but that it provides no guidelines for appropriate action. The essential ingredient of rationalization is distortion to protect ourselves. This distorted perception leads to the identification of the wrong elements to change. Typically, managers who are rationalizing may want to change others, or perhaps the technology, when they really should change themselves.

The best tipoff to rationalization in ourselves or others is the too perfect, too logical, or too consistent explanation. Life is fairly complex, and somewhat tentative explanations are what we usually must use. The rationalization, however, is usually a logical masterpiece. All the bits fit together to make a perfect cover-up story. Another tipoff is the insistence with which the rationalization is offered as an explanation. Shakespeare illuminated this with, 'The lady doth protest too much, methinks.' Winston Churchill is said to have sometimes written in the margin of his speeches 'WPS'. It meant 'weak point—shout.'

Projection ('It's you, not me')
Projection is attributing to others what is in fact in one's self. In

short, 'It's them, not me.' It operates primarily in those with low style awareness, those who do not know how they, in fact, behave. The mechanism is most clearly seen in delusions of persecution. A new manager may be in the process of making changes in a department. Not all will like the changes, and each will react somewhat differently. Subordinates might feel aggressive toward this new manager but, because of social training, may not express it or even be aware of it. By the mechanism of projection, the subordinates then may suspect the managers of having these feelings and, as an extreme, believe themselves victims of a conspiracy.

Such statements as the following may reveal projection at work: 'The production department is not to be trusted', 'They are wolves in sheep's clothing', and 'Every person has a price.'

Projection may be combined with rationalization with undesirable results. Some managers cannot accept and do not see the hostility in themselves. They may project this hostility onto others and see the others as mean and aggressive. These managers then may have to rationalize why the other managers act this way towards them. One form is to develop a belief that others want the job or are trying to get them fired.

Typical examples of projection are the deserter who sees others as lazy, the selfish person who complains that others do not share and low relationships managers who are concerned that no one seems to take an interest in them.

Projection leads to low managerial effectiveness because it can be maintained only at the cost of continually misperceiving social reality. Although such distortion is designed unconsciously to protect the manager, the effect, in the long run, may be the opposite.

Negative adaptation (accepting things as they are)

One of the most important characteristics of human beings is their ability to make a psychological adaptation to an essentially unpleasant situation. Defence mechanisms help them do this. On the detrimental side, many managers adapt to negative conditions in such a way that they lose their sense of perspective about what an ideal situation might be. They believe that they, their department or the company, are operating reasonably well or even perfectly. An objective view would not confirm this. One particular advantage of using competent outsiders for advice is that they can see the true situation. They have had no opportunity to make a negative adaptation to the situation.

Negative adaptation is likely to be less common with those managers who have frequent contact outside the organization, with those with much prior experience elsewhere or with those who are newly arrived. It can be reduced by a variety of training techniques designed to improve situational sensitivity and also by a sharper measure of managerial effectiveness.

Symptoms for causes (mistaking appearance for cause)
We are all 'natural born' psychologists and this leads us into many difficulties when diagnosing organization events. Most managers, in fact, customarily make a psychological interpretation of events rather than a sociological one, even when the sociological one is correct. The 'personality clash' diagnosis, for instance, in most cases is incorrect. The clash is often only a symptom and should not be diagnosed as a cause. To diagnose it correctly, it must be demonstrable that the managers involved will fight on the golf course or over a drink. If they are reasonably affable in these circumstances, it cannot be their personalities which clash. A more accurate diagnosis of the underlying cause might be 'role conflict'. That is, their respective jobs are so designed that clashes are inevitable.

As an example, suppose one manager is responsible for decreasing marketing costs and another for increasing sales; they do not report to the same superior and so have an ambiguous power relationship with each other. These managers, if committed to their jobs, will almost certainly fight. Is this best explained as personality conflict or role conflict? Clearly role conflict is the better explanation. The danger in calling it personality conflict is that both managers might be asked to take a human relations course and to be nicer to each other. Certainly this action would not get to the root of the problem, whereas a role-alignment meeting might.

Other such diagnoses which may be symptoms rather than causes are 'communication problem', 'empire building', and 'apathy'. Like 'personality clash', these are not always best explained by saying, 'People are like that.'

Lack of conceptual language (not talking the same language)
Managers who talk and work together need a common set of concepts which they share and agree on. Without such a set, intelligent discussion is hindered. Disraeli spoke for many when he said, 'If you want to converse with me, define your terms.'

One of the cornerstones of knowledge is the concept. A concept is simply a bundle of related ideas. To make talk more precise and economical we all use concepts. For example, we do not say that the car moved over a length 100 times 1000 times 1 metre every 60 minutes. We, instead, make an equivalent but shorter statement and say that the car's speed was 100 kilometres per hour. Without concepts (in this example, speed, kilometres and hours) language would be clumsy.

So it is with management. Concepts make discussion more precise and often much briefer. Arguments are not, then, over definitions but over the realities of the situation itself. Without the concept of style resilience, it is difficult to quickly make the point that style rigidity has its good side. Without the concept of personal effectiveness, it is difficult to explain how someone can be more effective and yet less effective at the same time.

The 3-D terms provide a conceptual language to make discussion and analysis more precise. The concepts are the fewest possible needed to consider effectiveness, situations and styles. They are usable to improve situational sensitivity because they force a focus on elements, activities or outcomes that might otherwise be ignored or misinterpreted.

Limiting value system (having one test for everything)

Some managers have what amounts to an intellectual rigidity by espousing a single value or point of view which colours and sometimes covers reality. They may believe that all problems are human ones, that all work must always be satisfying or that bigness destroys initiative. Whatever the view, when it is deeply held such a manager is compelled to distort reality to fit it. This produces very simple explanations, since everything is explained in the same way.

With a similar kind of simplified approach, some attribute the same motive to whomever it is they disagree with. An example of a motive might be 'power need'. But managers are not psychologists, and even psychologists do not agree upon which motives might be operating for a particular person in a particular situation. It is far safer and more accurate to observe and interpret behaviour, not motives, especially if we have a favourite motive we like to project onto others.

High levels of anxiety (being a worrier)

Some stage fright is usually a good thing. Moderate levels of anxiety tend to improve performance. Terror, on the other hand, usually does not.

As anxiety increases through low levels, performance also increases. There comes a point after stage fright level beyond which further increases in anxiety lead only to decreases in performance. Some persons are permanently anxious whatever the situation. They usually build up deep psychological defences to protect themselves from reality. Physical habits, or strong ideological positions about what is right, are less likely to become distorted as a result of high levels of anxiety. Perception, interpretation of motives and feelings about others *are* likely to become distorted however. Situational sensitivity in particular can be sharply reduced as anxiety increases. But this is precisely the time when it is needed most. Managers at these times are wise to turn to less anxious associates in order to read the situation; and this is what they usually do. Sometimes it is their spouse. Too infrequently it is their older children.

Learning from feedback

One way to improve your situational sensitivity is to learn from feedback you receive. It might be from a candid subordinate or colleague. Managers who want to be more effective seek feedback actively. They are not so concerned with the somewhat trite distinction of feedback into constructive and destructive categories. They are concerned whether it is valid and as quick as possible. They become very interested if the feedback they receive is different from their perceptions. Something must be going on; 'Here is my chance to learn.'

The feedback—learning cycle

Learning from feedback can be seen as a cycle continuously repeating itself. So long as the cycle is maintained, learning can continue. The two key elements in the cycle are making a sound situational diagnosis and obtaining feedback on the results of the actions.

The situational sensitivity cycle of Exhibit 16.2 has six steps. The sixth step leads into a repetition of the cycle.

Learning is a continuous process. It is difficult to suggest where it starts or ends. An effective manager is constantly making a diagnosis of the situation, using style flexibility or situational management, and assessing the effectiveness of such actions so that the nature of these interventions can be improved upon.

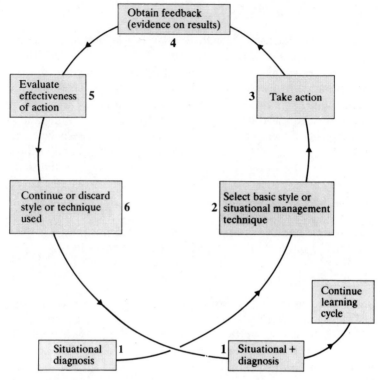

Exhibit 16.2   *Situational sensitivity cycle. Learning, like music, goes around and around*

How to analyse a situation

When you look at any situation you bring your knowledge, experience and perceptive skills to bear. On balance, this is probably the best way and the way you will continue to do so. In Chapter 18 on situational management many ideas will be given about how to introduce change, that is, situational management. Here we are thinking of how to analyse the situation that may need change, situational sensitivity.

The two remaining skills

This chapter was all about your situational sensitivity. Perhaps you have decided it is pretty high or perhaps you have decided it is not as

high as you would like. We now move on to the two things you can
do with your current level of situational sensitivity. You only have
two options. You either change yourself—style flexibility—or you
change the situation—situational management.

17. You and your style flexibility

Management must develop as broad a horizon as possible for every position, with guide posts along the way rather than rigid fences that hem the individual into a completely preplanned . . . existence.

Edward C. Schleh

People move in the course of their daily work from a role in one system to a different role in another system; and it is essential that this be recognized and that behaviour appropriate to the role be adopted if trouble is to be avoided.

Wilfred Brown

Once you have done your best to read a situation for what it truly contains you broadly have two choices. You either do a better job at adapting to the situation so that your managerial effectiveness increases—style flexibility—or you change the situation so that your managerial effectiveness increases—situational management. This chapter deals with the flexible response, while the next deals with situational management.

Most of both the psychological and management literature suggests that a manager with high flexibility is always likely to be a more effective manager. This is incorrect. Some managers change their minds and their behaviour to keep the peace. It might be perceived as being flexible but it is really drifting. Some situations require that a manager maintain a single appropriate style and virtually not vary it. One could hardly call this flexibility. It is clearly effective and we could call it resilience. Of course, maintaining a single style in a situation that does not require that style will lead to less effectiveness and we could call that rigidity. We need to be crystal clear about these differences. To help us, we need a new term. This term is flex. This refers to changing managerial behaviour, with no presumptions made about whether it is effective or not. Low flex and high flex behaviour are not more or less effective in themselves. Their effectiveness depends on the situation in which they are used.

To build this line of thought into the 3-D theory, four basic concepts are used to describe both the range of a manager's style behaviour and whether it is used appropriately:

- Style flexibility (appropriate high flex)
- Style drift (inappropriate high flex)
- Style resilience (appropriate low flex)
- Style rigidity (inappropriate low flex)

These four concepts can be represented as shown in Exhibit 17.1.

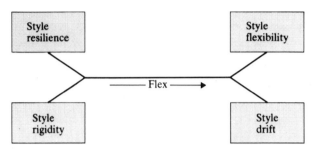

Exhibit 17.1   *The four basic concepts of flex*

The key dimension shown in Exhibit 17.1 is flex. That is, changing one's managerial behaviour. There are four possible outcomes of low and high flex as shown. These outcomes depend upon whether the high or low flex is appropriate to the situation.

So, while this chapter rather naturally espouses flexibility and links that to managerial effectiveness you must keep in mind that this is not true in every situation. Some situations may require the opposite. It is in those situations that low behaviour variation is used and situational management is used instead of style flexibility.

Flexibility and drift

If high flex managers are in a situation where their wide range of behaviour is appropriate, they are seen as having style flexibility. They are perceived as oriented to reality, sensitive, adaptive and open minded.

Even with little ongoing change about them, managers sometimes find they need to have high flex in the apparently unchanging job they have. As a manager supervising 10 people you might easily find that two work best when left alone, two need continuous direction, three need to be motivated by objectives, and the three others need a supportive climate. So, in the space of a day you as an effective manager may well use all four basic styles when dealing with such a variety as a dependent subordinate, an aggressive pair of coworkers, a secretary whose work has deteriorated and a superior interested only in the immediate task at hand. Obviously, to try to use a single basic style in these situations would lead to low effectiveness to say the least. To the extent the organization and technology allow individual treatment, high flex and sensitive managers could satisfy the demands of all these different situations and so achieve maximum effectiveness.

Many positions demand high flex because they require managers to deal with several different kinds of people or groups. The head of a voluntary agency could have to deal with a hostile or friendly board, a tough central fund-raising organization, professionals, volunteers, the press, the general public, and immediate subordinates. If one viewed this position as a whole at one time the total flex demanded would be very high indeed.

Whenever the topic of high flex is discussed, you may ask, 'Is high flex really role playing?' The suggestion is made that role playing is not being yourself or that it is somehow manipulative. The use of high flex is the ability to play a large number of roles, or use several styles, which is the same thing. Such high flex is best seen as using various parts of yourself as appropriate.

If managers continually change their style and so use the same high flex in a situation where wide ranges of behaviour are inappropriate, they will be seen as having style drift. They are perceived as yielding, unpredictable, and perhaps too sensitive.

Resilience and rigidity

If as a low flex manager you are in a situation where your narrow range of behaviour is appropriate, you are seen as having style resilience. You are perceived as self-confident, orderly, stable and consistent. Style resilience is not a popular subject for many management educators. It clearly should be taught, however, and given a positive value. While there is conflicting evidence, some studies do appear to indicate that subordinates are more likely to be satisfied with any particular style as long as they know what it is. They are less satisfied when they perceive no particular consistent style. Predictability, resilience, and subordinate satisfaction often go together. High flex managers succeeding low flex managers often find that their attempts to 'loosen things up' are not as rapidly successful as they had expected. Their subordinates' expectations about how they should behave inhibit their introduction of managing with a higher flex.

Many situations demand qualities associated with resilience. Managers who want to be flexible about everything they do will not last long. The modern organization is a recent and almost wondrous social institution. Its continuity and effectiveness, in part, is based on stability, predictability, and reliability. Its growth may, however, depend on quite different qualities. Obviously an appropriate mix of qualities associated with resilience and flexibility must be sought.

As a low flex manager you may find yourself in situations where a much wider range of behaviour is appropriate; you are then seen as having style rigidity. You will be perceived as having a closed mind, as intolerant and unsociable and as resisting change.

Much light can be thrown on the nature of resistance by referring to carefully controlled experiments. What follows may be seen by some as an extreme or unusual example. It is neither. It mirrors precisely what happens concerning resistance in organizations large and small. The experiment involves a fish tank almost filled with water with a glass partition in the centre, a big fish on one side and small fishes on the other side (Exhibit 17.2).

In this experiment, then, the big fish is separated from its natural prey, the small fish, by a glass partition. It can see them but cannot get at them. What happens, quite routinely, is that the big fish

Unfreezing needed here

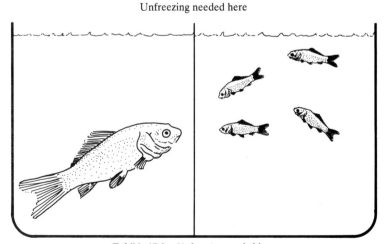

Exhibit 17.2 *Unfreezing needed here*

attempts to get closer to the small fish but continually bumps into the glass partition. After doing this a few hundred times the fish gets rather sore and stops doing it. So far what has happened is fairly obvious. What happens next is not. The glass partition is removed, the small fish surround the big fish and the big fish makes no attempt to eat them. The big fish, in fact, dies of starvation in what is a sea of plenty. It has learned only too well that the small fish are unavailable and that if you try to reach them pain will result. It has difficulty in unlearning what it has already learned so well. The big fish has been conditioned into not being able to learn or respond to a new situation. This experiment reflects precisely what is observed routinely in planned change programmes. Management thinks it is a good idea to 'remove the glass'. This may be their wish to introduce a new climate or new methods in the organization. Other managers in the organization, most having been around for a long time with a different system, have learned only too well to 'not go after the smaller fish'. Top management may initiate training courses, wave flags or give speeches all concerning the fact that they have removed the glass but the middle managers simply do not believe it and do not respond. Their problem is that they have some unlearning to do because the prior learning was so good. Not learning but unlearning. In short, they need unfreezing. They need to see what is really in their current changed situation rather than what used to be there.

Four checklists

The four checklists given in Exhibits 17.3 to 17.6 will help you gain an understanding of four concepts, style flexibility, style drift, style resilience and style rigidity. You might look at the four lists and check off the words you think apply to you and reflect some things you might want to try and change in yourself.

Style flexibility checklist	
Reality-oriented	Colleague orientation
Optimistic	Fair
Objective	Situationist (looks outward)
Other-directed	Adaptive
Sensitive	Open-minded
Collaborator	Socially adjusted
Tolerant	Experimental
Interdependent	Participator at times
Involved	Uses all basic styles
Team player	Practical

Exhibit 17.3 *Style flexibility checklist*

Style drift checklist

Uncommitted	Many promises
Procrastinator	Dependent
Disorganized	No self
'Yes' not 'no'	Compliant
Indecisive	Conforming
Yielding	Unpredictable
Inconsistent	Erratic
Misses deadlines	Helpless
Avoids adversity	Too sensitive
Gives lip service	Avoids rejection

Exhibit 17.4   *Style drift checklist*

Style resilience checklist

Will power	Firm superior
Tough-minded	Tolerates stress
Headstrong	Makes quick decisions
Simplifies issues	Follows orders
Self-confident	Stable
Clear goals	Systematic
Individualist	Disciplined
Orderly	Decisive
Persistent	Reliable
Good subordinate	Fulfills commitments

Exhibit 17.5   *Style resilience checklist*

Style rigidity checklist

Status-oriented	Resists change
Authority-oriented	Unresponsive
Control-oriented	Poor coworker
Prejudiced	Brittle
Closed mind	Limited responses
Intolerant	Overcontrolled
Inhibited	Unsociable
Poor listener	Rejects subordinates
Dogmatic	Self first not reality
Low self-insight	Personal blockages

Exhibit 17.6   *Style rigidity checklist*

Are you a naturally flexible manager?

There is little question that some managers are naturally more flexible than others and this is related, to a degree, to their personality. It is also true that increased flexibility is easily learned. Four personality characteristics underlie high flex behaviour. You might consider yourself as regards each one of them.

- High ambiguity tolerance (comfortable in unstructured situations)
- Unconcern with power (not control oriented)
- Open belief system (few fixed ideas)
- Other-directed (interested in others)

High ambiguity tolerance (comfortable in unstructured situations)

High flex types have a high tolerance for ambiguity. They are comfortable in an unstructured situation where one or more of the past, present or future are ill defined. They are not too threatened by rapid, unexpected changes. Not ones for paperwork, they see this as unnecessarily structuring a situation best kept loose. They favour short reports, loose ground rules and open-ended planning and scheduling. It is important to them to maintain a friendly, easy atmosphere where the 'old boy' approach is used more than 'standard operating procedures'. Approaches that could be characterized as 'right or wrong', 'black or white', 'go–no-go', and 'win–lose' are foreign to high flex managers.

Unconcern with power (not control-oriented)

High flex managers will often listen more to subordinates than to superiors because they are unconcerned with power. They generally favour flattening the status and power differences between levels and usually avoid displays of status symbols. They are in favour of most forms of participation. High flex managers are sensitive to the way things are. They see good management as the art of the possible. They would prefer to have things develop and flow naturally rather than go one step at a time or be dramatically restructured.

Open belief system (few fixed ideas)

High flex managers are open minded. They are ready to see new points of view and to expose themselves to influence. They could easily hold a particular view on one day and change their minds, in the light of new evidence, a day later. They are more concerned with full knowledge than in having their prior beliefs confirmed. They are less likely than others to take extreme positions for or against anything. They have a capacity to accommodate a wide range of viewpoints and do not feel they must make a successful synthesis of them.

Even when unable to accept another point of view, they will always listen to it, usually contemplate it seriously and often live comfortably with it, although it may be contradictory to their existing belief system. They are usually open to new inputs from any source. They are on a continuing search for maximum contact with their environment and are thus open to influence. This openness leads them to drop prior methods with ease. Not tending to hold extreme, fixed views, they argue less vehemently than others. They are tolerant of others holding opposite views. If they have to change their minds, they can do so easily. They are, therefore, as much interested in hearing other views as in pushing their own.

To have high flex, managers must have few intrusive personal needs. They must not have a need to do things in one way, to have a particular relationship with others, to live according to a particular ideology or to accomplish a particular thing.

Other-directed (interested in others)

Their openness to influence and their unconcern with power make the high flex type a team member. They want to be involved in analysis, planning and decision making with others. They seek collaboration with their coworkers and are willing to accommodate a group view rather than maintain their own. They thus are usually more prepared to work for a consensus decision than for a vote. They look for that creative solution or synthesis that everyone will accept. In fact, they find it a challenge to work for such a solution which combines all views, even though the final decision may have some ambiguous elements.

High flex managers tend to get involved with people as individuals, not just as subordinates or coworkers. They do not see others as bounded by their role. They are sensitive to individual differences and want to respond to them. They sometimes find themselves involved with another manager's home problems. They do this not because they are inquisitive or have high relationship orientation but because they are interested in a variety of inputs and thus look at the total person rather than at a human frame bounded by a job description.

Both high flex and low flex types can be seen as fair to others but for different reasons. High flex types are fair owing to their willingness to consider all points of view.

Low flex types are fair because they want to treat everyone equally and because they want to lower the ambiguity of the situation. The high flex type is generally more concerned with fairness to the individual, the low flex type with fairness to a particular social system as a whole. The high flex type tends to be sensitive to the relationships orientation elements in a situation, the low flex type to the task orientation elements.

High flex demands

Some managerial positions make high demands on flex so that a variety of basic styles must be used to produce effectiveness.

Job characteristics which usually demand high flex include:

- High level management
- Loose procedures
- Unstructured tasks
- Nonroutine decision making
- Rapid environmental change
- Manager without complete power
- Many interdependent coworkers

Very few jobs possess all the above-listed characteristics, but the following positions, having one or more of them, tend to make higher than average demands on flex:

- Senior manager
- Personnel manager
- Service function co-ordinator
- Research administrator
- Manager of staff department
- Supervisor
- University CEO

The more senior the manager, the more important high flex is likely to be. No administrative problem repeats itself in every detail. The higher the level, the more complex and diverse successive problems are likely to be. In many policy issues, the personality of the shaper has an enormous influence. It is then that flex can be of the utmost importance. Senior executives are continually encountering exceptional circumstances which fall outside established patterns of solutions. It is how they handle these situations that most determines their overall effectiveness.

High flex managers in a low flex organization may not be allowed to manage effectively, and if they do, they could get fired.

As a flexible manager you are perceived as having few personal needs or biases which might lead you to interpret wrongly the real world. You are reality-oriented, and this reality guides your action.

You are not led to analyse a situation in terms of how you think things should be. Rather you read a situation for what it is and for what can reasonably be accomplished. You seldom identify with lost causes but more often with objectives being achieved. As a flexible manager you are essentially an optimist about yourself and about the situation. Often you see things you do not care for but know that with time and appropriate behaviour the situation can be changed.

As a flexible manager you recognize that you live in a complex world, you are aware that a wide range of responses are necessary in order to be effective in it. You are very sensitive to other people and are not only sensitive to their differences but accept the differences as normal, appropriate and even necessary. You are trusted and believe that your proposals for change are based on improving overall effectiveness and are not intended simply to satisfy your own needs in some way.

As a flexible manager you spend more time in making decisions and less time in implementing them. You are concerned with method of introduction, timing, rate of introduction and probable responses and resistances. In spending more time on deciding how to implement decisions, the implementation period is shortened considerably. You seldom make snap decisions. As a flexible manager you use team management when appropriate. This gives you an ideal opportunity to use your flexibility.

Rapid changes do not make you unduly anxious. They bring temporary ambiguity which as a flexible manager you can tolerate easily.

You are likely to be willing to experiment with changes that have only a moderate chance of success. You know the world is complex and recognize that any change may bring unanticipated consequences so you are prepared to test a large number of ideas.

You are willing to accept a variety of styles of management, varying degrees of participation and an assortment of control techniques. Appropriateness is your only test.

In the course of a few hours, you may have used a variety of basic styles as a flexible manager. You adapt your style to what is then demanded. You use participation at times, and at other times you do not.

Why you may resist becoming more flexible

Quite apart from your personal defences there are many other explanations of why you may resist change in yourself, namely:

- No direction to change
- No skills to change
- No pressure to change
- Known is safer
- Personal effectiveness
- Shell shock
- Prior learning

No direction to change

Resistance to change often arises simply because the type of change desired is not specified clearly enough. It helps little to ask, implore or demand others to change if you are not clear on the exact nature of the changed behaviour required. Often, the unwritten desired direction is 'Change to whatever I want at the time.' In some settings this might be useful but in normal settings it is not common and normally less effective. As an example, the change request to 'improve communication' contains really no information on direction of change. Does this mean more talk, less talk, more memos, less memos, communication upwards, communication downwards, communication laterally, listening, more speed reading courses needed, more speed writing courses needed, more basic language courses needed, more use of the telephone, less use of the telephone, longer meetings, shorter meetings? Surely, the point is made.

Other examples of quite useless direction for change concern such statements as 'Let's make the organization more participative or more 9.9 or more Theory Y.' These statements contain no useful information. All this is why planned change must start with the notion of planned change objectives and how to measure these objectives. The whole point is to give change direction a high degree of specificity. Without this, planned change must stop dead in its tracks because everyone does not agree on what changes are being considered.

No skills to change

Change sometimes fails because managers are not provided with the skills needed to implement the change. Perhaps the new corporate planning scheme requires that managers have an increased ability to make a plan. It may well be desirable to arrange that every manager has a one- or two-day course on planning which might include, for instance, being competent at critical path analysis, at programme evaluation review technique, or at some other technique. Performance appraisal schemes often fail because they are introduced simply as a form which is distributed and managers told, essentially, to 'get on with it', rather than being formally exposed to a one-day course, probably using video tape feedback, which enables them to practise their use of the form and all that it entails on strangers before they use it with their subordinates. If one needs to make an organization more participative it might well be a good idea to offer managers a short one- or two-day course in listening skills or in participative meeting skills. Again, it is advisable to give them an opportunity to learn in a neutral and safe environment before they apply it on the job.

No pressure to change

In addition to directionality and skill level the successful implementation of change requires some pressure of some kind. In its starkest terms it might be financial rewards for successful behaviour change and financial punishments for no behaviour change. More often the pressure arises from a clear message from management that they want the change and are quite determined to see it implemented. Other pressures for change may be created by talks, meetings and system changes. The single best pressure always is that top management is seen to be supportive of the change and, as it applies, to be directly engaging the change itself.

Known is safer

It is quite common for an effective manager to resist change. The effective manager resists change because of the danger that in making a change the present good level of effectiveness might be decreased. In fact, the simple truth is that change introduction often results in a short term decrease in performance while new skills are being learned or while errors in introducing the change are being weeded out. Think of your own situation and some skill which you acquired too late. Perhaps you waited too long to become computer familiar. You thought that the time taken to learn it would lower your effectiveness with other things. Perhaps you took too long to become really able with a dictating machine. You were concerned that the time taken to learn it would detract from your effectiveness. It is important to understand that a manager who is effective and who resists change may be doing so simply because of fear of lowering the good standard of performance at the moment.

Personal effectiveness
While the approach so far has taken a fairly understanding view towards resistance, it can of course arise from purely selfish motives. If one is primarily interested in personal effectiveness—that is, meeting one's own personal rather than organization objectives— one may well show high resistance to proposed changes. If one is unduly concerned with one's own position, power, possible career route, size of office, work arrangements, numbers supervised and a host of other things, and puts these first, then it is natural to expect a higher resistance to reasonable changes which would improve organization rather than personal effectiveness. The best way to deal with this issue is to raise it with one's colleagues. The question that comes naturally is, 'Are you objecting to this change for reasons of managerial effectiveness or for reasons of personal effectiveness?' This is a routine question in organizations with good teamwork and candour.

Shell shock
Shell shock, in military medicine, applies to a psychological malfunction wherein the individual cannot cope with the existing unthreatening reality because of lingering feelings about an earlier shocking reality which was impossible to handle. Things are not quite that bad with most organizations, but they sometimes occur; otherwise, why would people involved in change frequently have heart attacks or ulcers, or become alcoholics? All of these can be seen as aspects of shell shock. Some companies pride themselves on being abreast of every new idea in management, and this obviously can be healthy, depending to what extent it is carried. But, if in an organization one year it is job enrichment, the next year quality control circles, the next year management by objectives, the next year participative management, and so on, then one may reasonably expect that the amount of change will be so great that it will be impossible for most managers to deal with it, and more important,

integrate its variety into some sense. Surely, this is an under-standable reaction. Planned change should involve a single compre-hensive set of ideas over a period of time long enough for them to be integrated into the ongoing life of the organization.

Prior learning
This refers back to the fish experiment. Some people cannot change because they have learned the wrong things too well. This is sometimes called trained incapacity. It is the most important example of the need for unfreezing.

Will you increase your flexibility?

You can think about your flexibility in terms of the basic styles. Is your behaviour range so narrow, as represented in Exhibit 17.7, that you are in one corner, as shown, or in another? Or do you have a broader behaviour range, as presented in Exhibit 17.8, with some capacity to use at least three of the basic styles?

From Exhibit 17.8 alone we cannot say whether the manager is more or less effective. We do know the manager has the capacity to use three styles. If one or more of those styles is effective in a situation then we would use the label 'flexibility', and if not, we would use the label 'drift'.

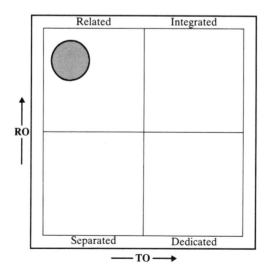

Exhibit 17.7 *A resilient or rigid manager*

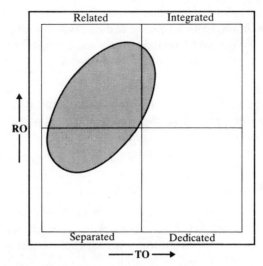

Exhibit 17.8 *A flexible or drifting manager*

Think about your results on the style test. If you had a double dominant basic style, such as missionary and developer, it is possible that your style variation is limited more or less to related. If you have a fairly flat profile it is probable that your style variation is fairly wide.

Can you become more flexible—really?
Think for a moment about the capacity for your own behaviour change. A rich relative has died, and in the will has left you an iron foundry. There is one key proviso. You must personally go and manage the iron foundry and if you change its current 1 per cent return on investment to 5 per cent return on investment within a 4 year period then the iron foundry becomes yours and you can do with it whatever you will. The estimated value with that kind of turnaround would be several times more than your expected income for the rest of your life. Do you think that you would be sufficiently motivated to attempt to improve the organization effectiveness of the iron foundry? While you probably have had no experience in this line of work do you think you might in fact have a good go at it and you might be reasonably effective if you put effort into it? Most people, like yourself, would say something equivalent to 'I will give it a go.'

Suppose, instead, you are asked to lead a university department of management. You are told that in the department there are lecturers all of whom are technical specialists in narrow subjects such as finance, tax, accounting, human relations, organization behaviour and statistics. You are told that they set their own curricula, that they set their own examinations, that they decide alone which students pass and which ones do not, and that it is not at all customary for heads of department to ever view a faculty member teaching; in short, you have little control. You are asked to improve the general organization effectiveness of the department and to represent the department well to the community. Do you think that this might be an interesting job for five years? Do you think that if you thought it was interesting you might try it?

The point with these two examples is that they would require completely opposite kinds of behaviour. The first would require a heavily dedicated task oriented behaviour and the second would require a highly related type of behaviour. You, in fact, believe that you could do either job if needed. One must conclude that you believe that you have a wide range of possible behaviour. It is not the capacity for behaviour change that is the limiting factor: it is the clarity of perception that makes it obvious that a particular change to a type of behaviour is needed. We all have an innate wide range of potential behaviour. We and others must learn to use it. We have no room for the resisting ones who claim that behaviour is difficult to change or cannot change.

There is no need to be pessimistic about changing your flexibility. The simple fact is that several excellent methods exist to overcome resistance. What is probably the most advanced method is a behavioural science type event called the 3-D Managerial Effectiveness Seminar. It has the following nine main components:

HOW TO IMPROVE FLEXIBILITY
- Theory: About behaviour
              About situation
              About effectiveness
- Awareness: Own behaviour
              Own situation
              Own effectiveness
- Skills: Situational sensitivity
              Situation management
              Style flexibility

To help managers change they need some cognitive framework. They need what is, in effect, a commonsense, easily understood language so they are all talking about the same thing in the same way. This language is obviously based on behaviour, on situation and on effectiveness. The behaviour may well consist of managerial styles, the situation or various situation elements such as technology and superior style which affect one's own behaviour and effectiveness. A very clear statement must be given about effectiveness itself. That is, what it is, how it is measured and how it should be improved. Another part of helping people to improve their flexibility should be an enhanced awareness of their own behaviour, their own situation and their own effectiveness. This, in effect, applies the theoretical knowledge to their own situation. The whole of this is to overcome distortion. These seminars start with a simple statement, 'The objective of this seminar is to help make you become more objective about your situation.' This may seem a strange way to start a seminar on managerial effectiveness but it is the best way if you follow the ideas here. Obviously, the final segment of the event must be skill improvement. What are the three skills of an effective manager? They must be the ability to size up situations for what they really contain—situational sensitivity; to change situations that need to be changed—situation management; and the ability to adapt to a situation which cannot or should not be changed—style flexibility. All this leads, logically, to improved managerial effectiveness.

What does becoming more flexible mean—really?
What is behaviour change really? Some, as a defence, imagine it is something to do with changing one's basic beliefs, changing one's lifestyle, moving from one role to another in terms of styles and other dramatic expressions. Effective behaviour change may involve one or more of these, but it normally does not. It is quite possible to achieve increments in managerial effectiveness with a relatively small amount of behaviour change which to many will be invisible. Here are some ideas:

WHAT IS BEHAVIOUR CHANGE?
- More or less planning
- More or less talking or memos
- More or fewer risks
- More or less consideration
- More or less participation

- More or less use of a style
- Higher candour
- Remove your desk

Some of the items on this list will seem to be quite minor but can be quite important. Some managers are mavericks, they wing it, they do not plan enough. Other managers are the opposite and like densely prepared bureaucratic schedules for everything, even when they are not needed and do not lead to improved effectiveness. Perhaps you should plan a little more or plan a little less. Perhaps you should talk more or less or use memos more or less. Think about what you are doing now and whether what you are doing is really the most effective method. You cannot possibly address this issue until you know what your 'outputs' should be and, to a degree, whether you are achieving them. Are you taking enough risks, or are you taking too many? One severe hindrance to behaviour change is the unwillingness to take any risks at all. But change of necessity involves risk taking, simply because we have not been there before. One must expect a short term decrement of performance with virtually any behaviour change. Perhaps you are showing too much consideration to others, perhaps too little. Perhaps you are using too much participation or perhaps too little. Think of the styles you use. Could you use some of them a bit more or a bit less? Should you be more candid about performance?

The point of all this is to indicate that important behaviour change to improve managerial effectiveness need not be dramatic. Overcoming resistance in one's self and in others is not necessarily high drama. It can often be things that are virtually invisible to the casual observer. There is no reason why we should not engage such behaviour change and no reason why we should not expect others to as well.

We need always to understand resistance but we need not always accept it.

18. You and your situational management

The fundamental qualities for good execution of a plan are, first, naturally, intelligence; then discernment and judgment, which enable one to recognize the best methods to attain it; then singleness of purpose; and, lastly, what is most essential of all, will—stubborn will.

Marshal Foch

- Those who make things happen.
- Those to whom things happen.
- Those who watch things happen.
- Those who don't even know that things are happening.

L. Appley

The essence of this last chapter, on situational management, is overcoming resistance to change. To a degree some of this resistance may be within yourself in that you are unwilling to exercise the situational management which would lead to managerial effectiveness. However, the presumption is that most of the resistance is in others and that you, as a manager, need to overcome it. Chapter 17 on style flexibility raised many issues concerning resistance, with the main focus being your own resistance to being more flexible. Obviously, all of those arguments also apply to others. In thinking about situational management and resistance in others do consider all you have just considered about yourself when thinking about your own flexibility. People tend to resist change instinctively based on both conscious and unconscious fears. Overcoming resistance to change is the effective manager's stock in trade.

Most common errors

Most of the possible errors in situational management have been discussed or inferred already. Some, however, occur much more frequently, and are more serious, than others. They are:

- Human aspects only
- Technical aspects only

- No information about change
- No planning of introduction
- No benefits
- Seen as personal
- Suppression of resistance
- Meeting force with force

A sole emphasis on the human aspects of change may lead to the changes being distorted from the original plan or may lead to no change at all. Overemphasis on the human side is sometimes induced by human relations training courses. Managers then become either overparticipative or guilty about the methods they have to use.

At the other extreme is a sole emphasis on the technical aspects of change. Engineers and systems department managers are among those who have been most guilty of this in the past. This kind of emphasis can lead to the most extreme personal resistance of all. This resistance leads either to still more impersonal pressure, to compromise, or to an abandonment of the project.

A widespread error, and one capable of a simple solution, is lack of planning of the method of introduction. This planning has nothing to do with the actual change itself but solely with the way it is introduced. A new method might have cost several million dollars to design and purchase, yet not even a single employee-year, nor even a month, is spent on ensuring smooth implementation. How much time should be spent? What is an appropriate situational-management design-budget percentage? In most firms it is zero. They think that a plan on paper is a short step from a plan implemented. It is not.

All change has associated benefits for the worker, manager, or organization as a whole. In the long run those working in the organization will gain if the organization gains. The benefits of some change may simply be survival, but benefits, in some form, are always present. Even though they may not be individual benefits, they should be stressed rather than ignored.

Sometimes change is resisted simply because it is seen as a result of a personal whim. This kind of objection is unlikely to be raised about the manager at the top of a profit centre. It is very likely to be raised about staff people who are seen as empire builders or about very ambitious managers who appear interested more in personal than in managerial effectiveness.

No normal manager prefers to use coercive means to suppress

resistance, yet most managers have and know they will again. There is no argument for suppression unless all else has failed. If absolute time limits are near and if others may suffer because of increased danger or the possibility of adverse economic consequences, then the method may be condoned. Suppression methods are familiar to all and include threats of punishment, offers of bribes, threatened termination, and the threat of cancellation of concessions already offered. These methods are not recommended unless others have failed or unless special conditions prevail because they can easily lead to increased resistance. If handled properly when they must be used, they can lead to increased respect.

It is unwise to interpret deep resistance as an attack on the manager or on the changes that the manager wants to implement. The resistance may simply be an instinctive or learned reaction to something strange. If so, it is unwise to meet force with force because it may turn what was simply an initial objection to a lasting resentment.

Ten tested techniques to overcome resistance

In order for things to be changed, resistance to change must be overcome. There are ten techniques by which this may be accomplished. They are easy to learn and just as easy to use. Most of them amount to common sense. All of them are well tested. They are as follows:

THE TEN TECHNIQUES
- Diagnosis
- Mutual objective setting
- Group emphasis
- Maximum information
- Discussion of implementation
- Use of ceremony—ritual
- Resistance interpretation
- Effective feedback to others
- Appropriate rate of change
- Changing the work system

The first three of these are specifically designed to give those affected by the change an opportunity to have some influence on the direction, nature, rate and method of introduction of the change. Giving those affected by it some control over the change enables them to become involved with it, to express their ideas more directly and to be in a better position to propose useful modifications in the proposed change if it should appear necessary to them.

Diagnosis

Resistance to change may be reduced if a diagnosis of the situation is first made by those affected by the change. The process of making the diagnosis leads to an increased awareness of what is wrong and this in turn can lead naturally to steps to change the situation. The diagnosis may be in the form of a work team discussing the question, 'What are the major problems we could solve if we worked together to solve them?' This kind of question has been used repeatedly with success at all levels of management. It is not only the ultimate diagnosis that the question produces that is important. The actual process of making the diagnosis itself leads to a profound 'unfreezing' by bringing people together to discuss certain things about their department that they have never discussed before. In such discussions they often gain new perspectives on old problems. They sometimes come to see that they themselves are the prime cause.

Mutual objective setting

Resistance to change is reduced by the use of objective setting by those instituting the change and by those affected by it. Much resistance is simply based on a misunderstanding about the true aims of the change. Once the aims have been set and agreed upon there is usually a straight road to their achievement. Objectives set by those affected by the change are generally more ambitious than those set by those not so involved.

Bargaining is a lower but often necessary form of mutual objective setting. It is a frank exchange based on, 'We will do this if you do that.' It is particularly useful and may be the only method to use with union militancy or in situations where hostility has led to poor communication. Bargaining is not necessarily a display of weakness, it may be an acceptance of reality. Bargaining usually leads to compromise. At its worst bargaining leads to obstinacy on both sides and a consequent win–lose approach to the final decision. But conditions can at times be created where it leads to a better decision than either side previously considered.

Group emphasis

Management training is now moving more and more to a group or team emphasis. It is becoming clear that the individual group member in isolation can have little influence without the whole-hearted co-operation of the others. The best way to obtain this is to train the managers as a team so that all ideas are team ideas and the team is committed to them as a unit. Some managers say that the first thing to do with an idea is to separate it from the manager who first thought of it and make it group property.

Resistance to change is reduced if the group is made the focus of change rather than the individual. Group decision making has a powerful control over the deviant member who is holding up the group. Groups develop powerful standards for conformity and the means of enforcing them. In the same way that a group can set up work norms to inhibit change, it can set up norms which facilitate it.

As with any technique there are times when group decision making is appropriate and times when it is not. For example, it should never be used when management has, or should have already, made up its mind. In fact, it can be used only when both sides have something to gain. Also, it can only operate when a group or potential group actually exists.

These first three techniques of diagnosis, mutual objective setting and group emphasis all involve participation in different aspects of the change. The term 'participation' itself was not emphasized as there is so much misunderstanding about it and disagreement over what it means. In the three techniques discussed there is no promise made that management will accept all the ideas suggested and there is no need for such agreement. The techniques can be used quite successfully when management says in effect 'This much is decided—what are your thoughts on the rest? We will consider all your proposals but cannot guarantee to accept them.'

The success of such methods as these depends on the extent to which they are seen as legitimate, honest and likely to be successful. While it can be done, it is difficult for a company to start too suddenly to use these techniques in situations where they have never been used before. A certain degree of trust is important and a certain degree of skill in implementation is crucial. Needless to say, managers cannot use these techniques if they have already finally settled on a course of action. To do so is both dishonest and folly. You cannot fool all of the people all of the time, and it only takes one to tell the rest. Pseudo-participation is time wasted for everyone and clearly inappropriate if a degree of appropriate participation could have been used instead.

Maximum information

When involved in any change, management goes through four distinct steps:

1 Recognizes change needed
2 Decides on ideal state
3 Designs method of implementation
4 Implements change

These should each in turn lead to four appropriate announcements:

1 That a change will be made
2 What the decision is and why made
3 How decision will be implemented
4 How decision implementation is progressing

Each of these can produce a possible resistance:

1 To thought of any change
2 To decision itself
3 To method of implementation
4 To changed state itself

When analysing a change in process, or when planning a change, these 12 elements should each be considered in turn. In particular, management should consider how well it is conveying the four separate elements of information required. There is a tremendous fear of incomplete information and people usually believe the worst.

The first piece of appropriate information, 'that a change will be made', is often omitted or left to rumour; the second, 'what the decision is and why made', is often made too tersely; the third, 'how the decision will be implemented', is often omitted and not enough thought, let alone communication is given to it; the fourth, 'how decision implementation is progressing', is seldom communicated, particularly when there is little that is good to communicate.

Maximum information is usually a sound policy after a change has been announced and sometimes, but not always, before it. Testing the wind with hints about forthcoming changes can sometimes provide useful pointers on the state of resistance or acceptance to the change. On the other hand, it can simply raise the level of anxiety and lead to wild rumours. Prior announcements should be crystal clear as far as they go but do not have to be complete. This vague sort of prior announcement or rumour is harmful:

'Some organization changes are coming.'

This kind of precise prior announcement is helpful:

'A reorganization to the top two levels of 'A' division will be announced on 1 September by the executive committee. The changes will be carried out during the following two months. The basic function of the division will remain unchanged.

Once a change has been announced the maximum possible information should be distributed about it. Resistance to change is almost always lower if the objectives, nature, methods, benefits and drawbacks of the change are made clear to all concerned.

Face to face announcements are better than the printed word. Not only do they personalize what may be seen as a depersonalized action but they also allow anxieties to be expressed clearly and perhaps dealt with on the spot.

Discussion of implementation

Discussion of implementation should be a part of the set policy of giving the fullest possible information. It calls for distinct treatment, however, as it is a most important step often overlooked.

Resistance to change is reduced if there can be agreement on the rate and method of implementation. It is as effective to have discussion on the way a change is to be introduced as it is to discuss the nature of the change itself. Such discussions will cover what the first steps should be, what the rate of change should be, what the appropriate sequence of changes should be and who should be involved in what elements of the implementation. When this method is used successfully it sometimes happens that the unit undergoing the change says to management, 'Leave us alone; come back in two weeks or two months and the changes will be in.' A wise manager accepts that kind of offer.

Use of ceremony—ritual

In primitive form, in western business society, the 'golden hand-shake' or gold watch presentation is a method of marking and facilitating a change of role from employed to retired. One problem with the ceremony is that it is essentially one of departure. Only those whom the retired person is leaving are present. This hardly facilitates entry into the community of the retired.

Life consists of a series of periods spent in different roles. Most of us follow a similar pattern. We are first infants, then school children, then lovers, then adults, then marriage partners, then parents. At school, at work or in some fraternal orders similar progressions occur. Some degree of ritual surrounds the passage of one role to another. The more important the role distinction is the more elaborate the ritual; witness the marriage ceremony.

When there are clearly established progressions from one role to another, change becomes much easier to accept. It means that you know that many people have done it before you. You know them, you are prepared for the future and you know what behaviour demands the next role will make on you. You know the conditions for entering the role and for remaining there. You know the meaning and use the various symbols, which might be a wedding ring or a big desk and a fitted carpet.

Some of the particular uses of ceremony and ritual for managers are:

- Pass on status—competence—power
- Prepare individual or group for change
- Provide a clear end and beginning
- Provide for orderly change
- Make change legitimate
- Emphasize individual responsibility to organization

A few more of the many occasions when one or more of these are accomplished and where ceremony and ritual are therefore useful are:

- Retirement
- Promotion

- Introduction of new coworker
- Introduction of new superior
- Introduction of new subordinate
- Move to new job
- Start of new system
- Reorganization

Ceremonies well used by a manager can serve to focus the importance of the ongoing institution and to underline the importance of individual loyalty to the institution and to the positions in it.

Clearly, managers need to learn how to use ceremony and ritual. Both can facilitate adaptation to what otherwise might be a painful adjustment.

Resistance interpretation

When people understand why they have been resisting a change, the resistance usually decreases or at least becomes more rational. Interpreting resistance with those who are resisting is a key step in psychoanalysis and in organization change consulting.

Resistance is seen as a symptom of something else, perhaps fear of the future or an unwillingness to give something up. The form the resistance takes is often an indicator of what the actual resistance might be. Seldom is the real reason given openly. Uncovering these reasons and discussing them can get at the true cause of the problem. Such interpretation of resistance is preceded or followed with some form of letting off steam. This may be in the form of a private or public 'beef' session.

Effective feedback to others

An important part of situational management and helping people change is to give feedback that can be heard. It is very easy to give feedback which no one listens to. Feedback of course is a two-way street but in this chapter we are thinking of your helping others through the use of the feedback you give. Effective managers use very short term feedback loops. They do not wait for the annual appraisal interview to let someone know what they think. They let them know as close to the time of the happening as possible. Experimental psychologists have proven, without any question whatsoever, that a very good way to improve performance is to give feedback on performance. If you want someone to get better, then let them know how they are doing.

Feedback may be classified by its timing, evaluative content, validity, and direction.

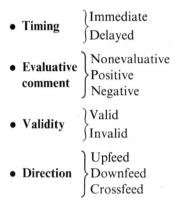

- **Timing** — Immediate / Delayed

- **Evaluative comment** — Nonevaluative / Positive / Negative

- **Validity** — Valid / Invalid

- **Direction** — Upfeed / Downfeed / Crossfeed

It is better for feedback to be immediate than delayed. The computer has already, and will even further, shorten the customary delay between managerial actions and their effects. Consider a situation where we could discover the effectiveness of our actions within minutes. The learning potential would be enormous, not to mention the early corrections to poor decisions. Clearly, managers should consider the timing of their existing feedback loops. How long does it take to know how a situation has changed, what it has become, or what the level of effectiveness is in it?

The best feedback is nonevaluative—that which simply 'tells it like it is'. Feedback, on which action must be taken, is less effective if feelings, positive or negative, are transmitted along with the information. For example, a subordinate is much more likely to respond to 'You did not meet your objectives', than to the same statement with the often unspoken override of '. . . and I do not like you because of it.' The first is nonevaluative feedback; the second is negative feedback. The terms 'negative' and 'positive', then, refer not to the content of the feedback but to the feelings that go with it. Unless specially designed to be otherwise, mechanical feedback devices or computer printouts are completely nonevaluative. Although difficult to accomplish, managers find that the closer they come to such feedback, the easier it is for others to really hear it and take action on it.

Feedback is either valid or not. Valid feedback may be negative, positive, or nonevaluative, but it is always accurate.

Feedback may come from any direction in an organization. To

indicate its direction, it is called upfeed, downfeed, or crossfeed. Downfeed almost always occurs plentifully; crossfeed and particularly upfeed have to be planned.

Appropriate rate of change

Very few social systems remain unchanged over long periods. Changes may be small and may be introduced slowly, but they do take place. The discussion of change, therefore, should be concerned not solely with its introduction but also with the rate at which it occurs.

In deciding whether to introduce change rapidly, the following factors should be considered:

- Is time important?
- What will be gained by speed?
- What was past custom?
- Will speed increase resistance?
- Can acceptance be sacrificed for speed?
- How would speed be interpreted?
- Are other changes still being assimilated?
- Must other changes be integrated?

There are some general arguments for both slow and rapid change. The arguments for slow change are:

- Usually produces less resistance
- Allows for gradual acceptance
- Will be seen as evolutionary
- Allows for greater understanding
- Allows for skill acquisition
- Changes can blend with others
- Changes and modifications in the proposed change, itself, will be easier
- Changes and adjustments to the method used will be easier

The arguments for rapid change are:

- Less time taken to reach ideal changed state
- Shorter adjustment period
- Only one basic adjustment required
- Less basic plan modification likely
- Adds impression of resilience

The speed of change is an important part of any complete plan for reducing resistance. It should be considered carefully along with the methods to be used.

Changing the work system

Most of this chapter has dealt with modifying the aspects of the human system but it might be the work system that requires situational management. This could take many different forms. It might be by reallocating outputs, changing the nature of information loops, making jobs bigger or smaller, adding or removing a person, changing the inspection process, and many, many more. Work can be divided up in many ways depending on the job to be done, and even particular jobs may be organized in different ways. A car can be assembled by a few workers or by hundreds or even thousands. A teacher may teach by lecture alone or with a team of others or by group methods or by the printed word alone. A worker may be given one operation to perform, perhaps an inspection, or may be given hundreds of sequential operations to perform.

Most assembly work may be accomplished by a single person or by many. A radio or TV set may be wired from single components by a single worker at a single workplace or by dozens or hundreds working sequentially. If errors are hard to discover and hard to correct and the total job involves many essentially similar operations and components, the work is perhaps best done by an individual.

Your style of situational management

These ten techniques can help you lower resistance to change. You may prefer to use one or two of them consistently or to use them all depending on the situation.

Situational management can be exercised using any of the four basic styles. It depends on the nature of the change you want to introduce. Obviously, if the change is to introduce some form of systemization then the separated style, oiled by the related style, would be a good idea. If you want to focus rather single-mindedly on results then the dedicated style would be appropriate. And so on. The style used may vary with the particular situational element being changed. As you know from Chapter 5, there are 20 of these. It is rather unlikely that you will change your superior by using the dedicated style. It is very likely you could change your coworkers by using the related style. An increasing level of creativity would have to come from either related or integrated styles, preferably integrated.

1 Superior	The person to whom you report
2 Coworkers	Managers of equivalent level or authority with whom you interact
3 Subordinates	Those who report directly to you
4 Staff advisers	Knowledge workers, usually with low authority and power, whose job it is to provide information and advice
5 Unions	Union representatives or members of unions
6 Customers	The purchasers of the company's products or services
7 General public	Anyone who is not an employee or customer of the company
8 Creativity	The production of ideas
9 Objectives	What you plan to achieve
10 Planning	The specific means whereby objectives are realized
11 Change introduction	The actual initiation of a new plan
12 Implementation	The actions taken to realize plans and decisions
13 Controls	Methods of monitoring actions so that adjustments can be made if necessary
14 Evaluation	Measurement of the effectiveness of action
15 Productivity	The level of the manager's output of those things required by the manager's superior
16 Communication	Receipt and transmission of information
17 Conflict	Disagreements
18 Errors	Things that go wrong
19 Meetings	Two or more people coming together to discuss something
20 Teamwork	Interaction between two or more people with high emphasis on both task and relationships orientations

Exhibit 18.1   *Which situational elements should you change?*

Exhibit 18.1 is a list of the 20 situational elements already discussed. Which do you think should be changed in some way to improve your managerial effectiveness? Check these. Then, against each one you have checked, list the basic style which you think is best to create the change you want. If you check several it might be a good idea to allocate 10 points over them to indicate their relative importance. You may wish to change everything at once but you cannot always do that. That is life, and work forever.

The main thing is, please do something to improve your managerial effectiveness. I did not write all this simply for my health, obviously. Over to you.

PART 5

Improving your effectiveness

The single chapter in this part outlines a training design which would be useful for those in an organization who are concerned with improving overall organization and managerial effectiveness.

19. How to improve your managerial effectiveness through training: (the managerial effectiveness seminar (MES))

This book has given you many ideas on improving your effectiveness. You may have read it on your own or used it as part of a training programme. This chapter outlines a formal way of improving managerial effectiveness through the use of a managerial effectiveness seminar (MES). Training managers, in particular, will find this chapter very useful as it will give them some training design ideas for improving effectiveness. Managers not in training roles will also find the chapter useful in that it gives yet another framework to thinking about improving one's own effectiveness.

As might be expected, the seminar is based on the theory outlined in this book. That is, the emphasis is on effectiveness, situation and style. The seminar has many practical types of exercises and activities which drive home what all this really means. You can then apply the entire theory to your own situation and activities. At the conclusion of the seminar you will be highly conscious of yourself as a key figure in a situation where effectiveness could be increased. You will become more open to change and see yourself as a key to improving effectiveness rather than leaving it up to others.

The MES is a six day, residential, instrumented laboratory. The seminar starts at 5.30 p.m. on the first day, and ends at 12.30 p.m. on the sixth.

How the seminar improves your effectiveness

The seminar improves your effectiveness by giving you more clear knowledge about effectiveness and by giving you skills that relate to effectiveness improvement. The seminar concentrates on these things:

- Improving your understanding of management concepts
- Improving your knowledge about effectiveness
- Improving your self-awareness
- Improving your three managerial skills
- Improving your teamwork skills
- Improving your on-the-job effectiveness

Improving your understanding of management concepts   Sometimes managers are less effective than they should be simply because they do not understand basic management concepts. Some of these, that appear to be quite standard terms, are widely misinterpreted. It is enlightening, though saddening, to find how in a single organization or in a single work team different interpretations are given to such concepts as participation, delegation, teamwork, autocracy and even objectives; obviously, there are many, many more. It has been demonstrated conclusively that simply a knowledge of what key terms mean in management can on its own improve effectiveness. Obviously, when these concepts and their definitions are shared by a team and then shared company wide, effectiveness must increase. Organizations need a common language if they are to improve effectiveness in an integrated way. Here we are again reminded of Disraeli's words, already quoted in Chapter 16: 'If you want to converse with me, define your terms.' All this may seem a little strange in a book which is clearly devoted to a behavioural approach, but while the book has indeed taken a behavioural approach in no way has it discarded the necessity for clear thinking first.

Improving your knowledge about effectiveness   The seminar emphasizes effectiveness as the central issue in management. One full day of the seminar is spent solely in each team reaching agreement on the effectiveness areas for each team member. It is really quite important that managers know that apparent, personal and managerial effectiveness are quite different. It is also very important for them to have confirmed their perceptions about these three terms by discussing actual situations and actual managers, possibly through case studies, to make sure things are fully understood.

It is surprising how many managers come to the seminar with the belief that for some reason their job is somehow unmeasurable and their job should not have clear outputs. Some jobs are continually changing. The best way to deal with this change is through a recognition of the change in effectiveness areas and the best people to do this are the managers whose positions impinge on the job.

Improving your self-awareness   This book has helped you improve your self-awareness. You may well see yourself quite differently and have thought of some things you want to do more of and some things you want to change. One important objective of the MES is to advance this learning even further. You now accept that a key step in improving your effectiveness is through better understanding of your own behaviour and its impact on others. Your seminar team members will spend a day with you on giving very frank views on the styles of everyone in the team. Some are slightly apprehensive about this before the seminar but the seminar is so designed that the day runs comfortably and well.

Obviously, through this activity, a lot is also being learned about giving and receiving feedback that can be hard. It is one thing to say that highly task-oriented managers tend to see relationships-oriented managers as less effective, but this may in fact be one of your distortions. The seminar will highlight your distortion and those of others and there are opportunities to discuss them.

Improving your three managerial skills   Up to now the MES has been described in terms of cognitive learning and not learning about self or about managerial effectiveness. Obviously, there is a heavy skill-building element in the seminar. These skills must be the three managerial skills of situational sensitivity, situational management and style flexibility. The seminar is so designed that there is a virtually continual opportunity to use all three skills and a virtually continual assessment of these skills by yourself and your team members and by seminar instruments. The seminar provides immediate feedback on your level of skills over a variety of activities, also immediate feedback from your team members on how you might improve as well as further feedback from team members on whether you did or not.

Improving your teamwork skills   One very important component of situational management is teamwork skills. That is, how to help a team get the best out of the team. Many managers think they are naturally good team members when in fact they are in the lowest 5 per cent of the population. They imagine that when they are keeping quiet they are really listening, though in fact what they are actually doing is thinking up new arguments. They think that the lowest conflict possible is best; however, this is not usually the best way to get a good decision. They do not understand consensus and always want a chairman who puts things to a vote. They simply do not believe that two heads are better than one and have no concept of synergy or how to get it. There are many, many 'tricks of the trade' in team skills. These are formally taught at the seminar and an opportunity given to practise them. Sometimes teams should work in a creative mode, sometimes in a purely procedural mode, sometimes in a bureaucratic mode and sometimes in an integrated way. These, of course, parallel the four basic managerial styles. So, direct transfer is made between styles of individual managers and team styles. You will learn, very quickly, at the seminar how to appraise the mode the team is in and how to change it. The teams put themselves under continuous assessment and review.

A major instrument is the team style diagnosis test which the team uses nightly to review its activities during the day. There are eight scales. One of the scales is conflict. The team spreads ten points over these eight statements, each representing a different managerial style. This is done for the seven other components as well.

It has been determined quite conclusively that the seminar effects are magnified when the actual work team meets in the months after the seminar to apply the seminar ideas to the work team itself. The whole point in management training is what is called transfer of training and the transfer is greatly facilitated when a superior and all immediate subordinates sit down to discuss their effectiveness areas and other things that impinge on their managerial effectiveness.

Improving your on-the-job effectiveness   Clearly, the sole way in which the effectiveness of an MES is to be judged is whether or not there are improvements in the job effectiveness of the participant. The seminar accomplishes this is several ways. Simply increasing clarity of thinking about effectiveness can, alone, improve effectiveness. Obviously, enabling managers to become much more aware of themselves and their impact on others, and of how to change themselves and others, can improve effectiveness. There are many additional techniques built into the seminar.

In the last half of the seminar participants are talking only about themselves and their real situation and how to improve it. A variety of diagnostic tools are provided, including tests of managerial and team effectiveness. The team approves a set of effectiveness areas which can be used as a basis for the job, a comprehensive management style profile arrived at jointly by the team and the manager involved, and various tests, that is, ratings of managerial, personal and apparent effectiveness and also the three managerial skills, with ideas on how to change those that should be changed.

Questions typically asked about the seminar

Managers interested in this seminar naturally have several questions. Here are some common ones, followed by their answers:

- What do I do each day?
- Is the seminar 'safe' for me?
- Will the seminar apply to me?
- What about managerial effectiveness in the organization?

What do I do each day?

The seminar can be seen as having five stages in learning.

Prework You will receive a prework kit. This consists of three texts, wall charts and a seminar workbook. The basic text is *Managerial Effectiveness* (Reddin, 1984). This explains the 3-D theory and shows how it is applied to improve effectiveness. The general seminar workbook contains questionnaires, style tests, effectiveness inventories, seminar tasks, case studies, team diagnosis instruments and other learning aids. Depending on your prior knowledge, capacity and dedication, seminar prework generally takes from 50 to 100 hours to complete.

Days 1 and 2 You will work in teams to deepen your understanding of the basic concepts relating to effectiveness. By the end of day two—Monday evening—you will have a thorough understanding of the prework and have a common language with which to approach the more complex aspects covered during the rest of the seminar.

Day 3 The effectiveness concepts are applied to a case study so their practical application is demonstrated and learned. Team building skills are also practised and reviewed. At the end of the third day team members evaluate the performance of their teams.

Teams usually engage in open and candid discussion on their performance. The skills to identify ineffective performance and to discuss it openly are rapidly built.

Day 4   This day is spent on effectiveness. You are provided with a sharp and objective view of your individual role in the on-the-job situation. You also receive the practical skills needed to define your own job and those of other managers in output terms. You will also get the confidence and practical skills needed to define effectiveness areas in an open team setting.

Day 5   The fifth day is spent on managerial behaviour. The objectives of this day are:

- To provide you with useful feedback on your own style
- To improve your skill in appraising the style of others
- To improve your skill in giving useful feedback
- To improve your skill in receiving feedback

Day 6   The last day concentrates on situation management. You will be provided with an opportunity to consider what personal changes you could make which would improve your managerial effectiveness in your on-the-job situation. You will also learn to give important practical guidance in a team setting. If the seminar is an incompany one then a senior manager will attend to receive feedback from seminar participants.

Is the seminar 'safe' for me?
Some managers are naturally concerned about the safety of the seminar for them. Perhaps safety is too strong a word but it is comprehensive. Some managers are concerned that their education is limited and that they have not read a book in years; they simply wonder whether they can handle a concept.

The truth of the matter is that those who feel they may not be up to it learn an additional big thing from the seminar, that they *are* up to it and can expect much more of themselves. The seminar is not an examination, it is a developmental, helpful experience.

Often teams bring out team results on various things but none of this is ever identified with specific individuals. Your team members will know your style well because they have worked with you for a week. Also, they will tell you what they think of your style, as you will tell them about their style. There is never ever any feedback to management or to other teams—ever. Again, the purpose is development not assessment. In any case, the theme of the seminar is that team members help each other to improve. In no way is criticism the objective. The seminar is also made safe by the nature of the team compositions.

Teams have normally from four to eight members. In a public seminar team membership is assigned, essentially, randomly. On an incompany basis the key rule is that no one on the team has a natural working relationship with others on the team on a day to day basis. In short, this elimates superior–subordinate and immediate coworker relationships. The whole idea of the seminar is to give team skills, natural feedback, consensus testing, complete resolution and many other things a chance to develop. This is better done with strangers than with those you are working with every day.

Will the seminar apply to me?
There is much evidence that the seminar has wide applicability. This evidence relates to levels, functions, ages, types of organization and countries.

The use of the MES across levels   The seminar has a demonstrated effectiveness at all managerial and supervisory levels. General Motors, for instance, uses the seminar from plant managerial level down to general foreman level. When the seminar is used as part of an organization development programme it is obvious that all levels of management and sometimes supervision attend the same seminar.

The use of the MES across functions   The seminar has obvious application across all management functions. Some organizations send their top 250 managers and in one case more than their top 1500 managers, through the full six-day residential seminar. Obviously, most types of functions must attend. No adverse effects, by functions, have been reported.

The use of the MES across ages   Age, young or old, is no deterrent to the effectiveness of the managerial effectiveness seminar. Managers of 21 and up to the age of 75 have fully participated. In one seminar in a family company the parents of 72 and 75 attended the seminar along with their children of about 40. An older manager of 64 came to a seminar staff member at the end of one seminar and said, 'I only wish I'd taken this many years ago.' He was not saying it was not effective for him—but that it could have been even more effective earlier.

The use of the MES across types of organization   Broadly, the seminar has been used to improve the effectiveness in organizations as diverse as production organizations, marketing organizations, military organizations, government organizations and virtually most types you might think of. In particular, the seminar has been used by Imperial Chemical Industries directors, General Motors plant managers, 35 employees of a 100 employee bakery, and 20 employees of a 125 employee brewery.

The use of the MES across countries   The MES has been conducted in these countries: Argentina, Australia, Belgium, Brazil, Canada, Eire, Ethiopia, Finland, Germany, Guyana, Jamaica, Kenya, Mexico, Netherlands, Norway, Singapore, South Africa, Spain, Sweden, Trinidad and Tobago, United Kingdom, United States and Venezuela.

What about managerial effectiveness in the organization?
The MES is used either as management development where the focus of change is the individual manager or for organization development where the focus of change is the organization as a whole.

Whether used for management development or organization development, the MES is best used on an incompany basis.

When large companies use the seminar simply as management development, they do not link it to any later team building or make any particular attempt to transfer the things learned back to the job. Their general assumption is that the climate of the firm can produce the necessary followup needed and what the seminar really has to do is to get managers unfrozen enough to engage their work situation on their own.

Internal staff   Most MESs are run by company staff members. Sometimes these staff members are drawn from the personnel training departments and sometimes from other line or staff functions. As a general rule, we find that our postseminar reaction forms show higher results when the seminars are conducted by internal staff, even though they were never trainers.

Seminar availability   The seminar is available on an incompany basis in any country at any time. The only limiting factor is language. The seminar is now translated fully into these languages: Dutch, Finnish, German, Norwegian, Portuguese, Spanish and Swedish.

Index